stuart dempster
and **dennis hay**

youth hockey
drills

SECOND EDITION

A & C Black • London

Dedication

For my wife Tan and daughter Natasha

Published in 2005 by
A & C Black Publishers Ltd
36 Soho Square, London W1D 3QY
www.acblack.com

Second edition 2009

© 2005, 2009 Stuart Dempster and Dennis Hay

ISBN 978 14081 0982 3

A CIP catalogue record for this book is available from the British Library.

Acknowledgements
Cover image © Alex Williamson
Illustrations by Mark Silver
Photo credits: pages 17, 47, 114 Matthew Lewis/ Getty Images; 30 Dibyangshu Sarkar/AFP/Getty Images; 39 Brendon Thorne/Getty Images; 55, 101 Jamie McDonald/Getty Images; 62 Paul Ellis/AFP/Getty Images; 66 Ezra Shaw/Getty Images; 71 Kazuhiro Nogi/AFP/Getty Images; 83 Viktor Drachev/AFP/Getty Images

Note: While every effort has been made to ensure that the content of this book is as technically accurate and as sound as possible, neither the authors nor the publishers can accept responsibility for any injury or loss sustained as a result of the use of this material.

Typeset in 10/12pt DIN regular
Printed and bound in Great Britain by Martins the Printers, Berwick upon Tweed.

CONTENTS

ABOUT THE AUTHORS

Stuart Dempster was born in Swindon, Wiltshire and is the former Scottish Champion at 400 m hurdles. He studied Sports Coaching at Heriot-Watt University, Edinburgh as well as at I.N.S.E.P., Paris; C.R.E.P.S., Poitiers, France; The National Academy of Sport, Karlstad, Sweden and in the former USSR by invitation of the Soviet athletics team.

As a coach he broke new ground by coaching the first Scot, Ken Campbell, to run under 14 seconds for the 110 m hurdles en route to becoming the first Scot to make the final in this event at the Commonwealth Games in 1994.

Having guided many athletes to national and age group records, Stuart has worked extensively in other sports particularly rugby, soccer and tennis, and of course hockey. He is the former National Athletics Coach for the Seychelles, and whilst Director of Coaching for Sport and Recreation Wanganui, Stuart became a key advisor to the New Zealand government's 'New Zealand Coaching Strategy' publication, and assisted with the content of the Coach Development Modules.

Stuart recently headed up a New Zealand/Australian consortium to enable a new sporting franchise to be established in New Zealand – The Victorian Athletic League. He also has a coaching consultancy business, Team You Coaching, which also includes corporate work by introducing a coaching approach to management in business.

Dennis Hay was born in Aberdeen, and studied Physical Education at Jordanhill College, Glasgow. He played international hockey for Scotland (1964–74) and Great Britain (1966–72) including at the Olympic Games in Munich. Dennis coached Scotland men in the Indoor European Cup finals (1974 and 1976), then Scotland women in outdoor World Cups (1983 and 1986). From 1985 to 1992 he was the coach to the Great Britain women's team who qualified for their first ever Olympic games in Seoul (where they were placed 4th), before winning a bronze medal in Barcelona. Retired from teaching, he is currently Director of Men's Hockey Coaching at Edinburgh University.

ACKNOWLEDGEMENTS

For this, the second edition of *101 Youth Hockey Drills*, I would like to acknowledge the assistance of the following in building the background from which this book has emerged.

Jenny Grassick, former Scotland Hockey captain, encouraged and gave me my first break into lecturing and age group working at Balerno High School, Edinburgh.

Chris Sutherland, former GB/Scotland Hockey international of MIM Hockey club, for having the courage and foresight to involve an athletics coach to look after his hockey team's fitness programme.

Louise Burton and Alan Hay (Scottish International Players) for feeding back to me what a hockey player actually requires in terms of fitness and movement skills.

John Lyle, my course leader at University, enthused us all and gave us the ability to think about new coaching concepts and processes.

Frank Dick, coach to numerous Olympic gold medallists from many sports. Frank always inspired me, gave me confidence and valuable advice.

Lastly but by no means least, Mr Joe Torrance and Em-orn Chaiyachart for giving me exclusive use of their condominium near Hua Hin in the Gulf of Thailand. This allowed me to attend to all the work required, in a beautiful and peaceful beach-side environment.

Stuart Dempster

I would like to acknowledge Anne, my wife, who understands.

Dr A. H. (Sandy) Innes. Sandy did more to help me, both with hockey and socially, than I knew at the time, but have since come to appreciate. He and Sylvia encouraged a whole generation of players and did much to push Scottish hockey forward while receiving little recognition for their work.

Di Batterham and Lynn Booth, the GB Manager and Physio, for all the long late-night discussions about hockey and whatever, in all sorts of places.

All the players who I have 'experimented' with on drills, exercises and tactics over the years. I hope that they mainly enjoyed it. I certainly enjoyed being with them.

Dennis Hay

FOREWORD

The expansion of your reservoir of exercises and activities is a never ending story. Whether you are a teacher or coach, committed to effectiveness and excellence in your role, there are three main reasons for the pursuit of that expansion.

First, it ensures that you will enrich lessons or training sessions with a variety of practice which will capture and maintain the interest and motivation of the young people whose steps through sport you lead. Next, it increases the probability that players' specific learning and training needs are successfully addressed through their years of introduction to hockey, and then of their development in the sport throughout their lives. Whether that lifetime is at leisure, club or elite level, it is critical that the fundamentals are correctly and robustly established. Finally, it affords stimulus to spark your imagination to introduce your own exercise and activity creations.

The resources for your reservoir are several. Coaching clinics, coach education practices, movies, articles, dedicated web pages and books are all extremely useful. The most valuable are those that reflect the quality experience of quality coaches: this is not only because what they give you is what to do and how to do it, but you will have confidence that they know why these exercises and activities work.

I believe that *101 Youth Hockey Drills* is one such valuable resource. Stuart and Dennis have an immense amount of experience under their belt in working with players from beginner to Olympian. Moreover, because they have absorbed the input of Jenny, Louise, Chris and Alan in checking out the drills variously from a teacher, coach and player's perspective, you have been guaranteed an exceptional book.

So now decide the results your team or teams are aiming for this year. Then determine what your players must achieve to deliver these results. Next, establish where they are now relative to that performance. Then plan how you will take the players from where they are now to where they have to be, breaking the year or season into progressive phases of development. Finally, digest what is here, then select where your choice of drill fits into the lessons or training units you have designed for these progressive phases.

The stages of player development in terms of their participative life are:

1 Train to train
2 Train to perform
3 Train to compete
4 Compete to learn
5 Compete to win

101 Youth Hockey Drills fits excellently into stages 1, 2, and 3 which is exactly where you come in.

I hope you enjoy this valuable resource and I wish you well in your work with the young people who are fortunate enough to have you as their teacher or coach.

Dr Frank Dick OBE
August 2008

INTRODUCTION

Be the best you can be

'In order to become a good player, first you must become a good athlete'

Pele (legendary Brazilian Footballer)

The reason people coach is for the benefit of the players. Through you I hope that this book can be of some assistance to the many aspiring hockey players out there who want to be the best that they can be. The process involved here does not necessarily mean that you produce young world-beaters at a very early age. Rather it is to give them all of the tools now with which to maximise their potential at a later stage. Indeed most of the world's top sports people were certainly not world-beaters at youth level.

The drills contained within these pages are a pointer to youth development.

Leading authorities on long-term player development agree that the window of opportunity for special development of loco motor (movement skill) through training the central nervous system is 8–14 years of age (FW Dick 1997, Bali and Hamilton 1998). At youth level therefore, coaches, teachers and parents must introduce training sessions and units, which are focused on developing the central nervous system as part of the young player's specific skills development. If this window of opportunity is missed, it cannot be fully recovered in later years.

In this book there are a variety of drills to assist in teaching players to move more efficiently and quickly. The importance of this cannot be overstated as players not in possession of these skills will use more energy, pick up more injuries and lower their potential ceiling of achievement as a result of moving ineffectively. In my opinion, the basic hockey-related movement skills must be introduced and developed in an enjoyable and challenging manner from the outset and must be constantly worked on during the players' progression through the age bands. It is then incumbent on the coach/teacher to set sessions up in as interesting and relevant a way as possible. The younger ones especially like to be learning in an interesting, varied, friendly and fun environment.

Working with this age group is one of the most satisfying areas of sport. Starting off with the 'rough diamonds' possessing minimal skill and knowledge, then gradually watching them mature into capable players able to perform at increasingly higher levels of competition is truly gratifying.

Both Dennis and I have experience in dealing with youth level players. Dennis has taught PE for many years in the 12 to 18 years age group, but has also coached teams from club level to Olympic level.

At world level, Dennis steered the GB Women's Hockey squad to a fourth place at the Olympic Games in Seoul, South Korea in 1988 and then on to a bronze medal in Barcelona four years later. Dennis Hay has to be regarded as one of the world's top hockey coaches; certainly no Great Britain coach has emulated this achievement since Barcelona.

I completed my thesis on child and youth development whilst studying coaching at Heriot-Watt University, Edinburgh. As a sprints/hurdles coach, having trained a Commonwealth Games finalist in Victoria, Canada in 1994, plus many sprint, hurdling and jumping champions and record holders, I was invited to assist Coach Chris Sutherland at MIM Hockey, Edinburgh as their fitness advisor. This enabled me to devise skill-based conditioning routines and develop hockey related movement skills capacity.

Many of the drills in this book are borne from my work at schools and clubs, as well as working with and talking to male and female international players about appropriate movement skill routines to help improve their game.

I hope that you will benefit from my experiences and trust that you will derive satisfaction from developing youths into more complete performers.

Stuart Dempster
April 2005

KEY TO DIAGRAMS

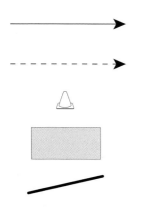

movement of player with and without ball

movement of ball only

cones or markers

goal or rebound board

lattes or sticks

DEVELOPMENT

There are very few examples of youngsters being stars at high school and then going on to be senior stars. Most gifted individuals also excel at other sports and activities. The fact that they participate at these other sports only helps them to achieve at a high level at their chosen specialist activity.

There is nothing better than to have your promising hockey players participate in and do well in other sports, as this will widen their skills base, provide a solid base of conditioning, enhance social skills and contacts and prevent injury. In particular they should be encouraged to do athletics, which is the basis of all sports, gymnastics, basketball, combat sports, dance and swimming.

Trying to get youngsters into one sport early will only lower their potential ceiling of achievement and is likely to lead to early retirement. In addition playing hockey year-round will contribute to burnout, as does placing players in higher age groups – let the youngsters develop a solid foundation and acquire a hunger for the sport beyond high school. When you consider that many sports possess athletes who have ended their successful careers in their late 30s, 40s and even 50s, there is surely no rush.

The coaching staff should endeavour to take a long-term approach, with the player's well being at the centre of the process. This may mean altering current practice relating to the number of games played annually for example. It will involve a shift in approach to the actual way we coach and it will also involve the player's parents as part of the process.

The adult ego will need to be kept in check, we are here to develop young players after all.

Approach to developing youngsters

1 Structured fun sports, downsized to fit the youngster.
2 Unstructured play with their peers.
4 Appropriate levels and volume of competition.
5 Participation in as wide a variety of sports and physical activities as possible.

FITNESS

Hockey is a fast moving sport requiring large amounts of running. It has been estimated that a player can cover between 8–10 kilometres during a senior game. The running required is at a variety of speeds, the player is required to get down low to hit a ball, or to take it off the opponent in a lunge type activity. They need to twist, turn, change direction, jump and have good grip on the stick in contact situations.

If you are a goalkeeper you need to be agile and explosive whilst wearing all the protective gear. In short, hockey is a multi-pattern sport which requires a great deal of athleticism.

When considering a fitness programme for youngsters, there are many elements to take into account. I would strongly advise a preventative approach getting all the players assessed for possible injuries BEFORE they happen. This approach takes a bit more time at the beginning, but pays handsomely down the track.

Let's consider the following study based on the main results of an injury study carried out by the National Collegiate Athletic Association (NCAA) between seasons 1998/9–2002/3.

The study found the following to be the main injury sites for hockey players:

1 Ankle sprains
2 Concussion
3 Head, neck and face (caused by contact with the stick or ball)
4 Hand, finger and thumbs (caused by contact with the stick or ball)

Basic functional strength and fitness is solely derived from what we call primal movement patterns and can help to prevent such injuries. All of the movements below can be developed by doing circuit training. Little or no equipment is involved in setting up circuit sessions and the creative and imaginative coach can make use of the local environment.

the primal movement patterns

1 Squatting
   Daily life Simple activities such as sitting in or getting out of a chair or car
   Sport Basic strength development often requires this training activity

2 Twisting
   Daily life Picking something off a floor and placing it on a table behind
   Sport Winding up and hitting a ball in hockey, a tennis serve, javelin throwing

3 Pushing
Daily life Opening a door, pushing a shopping trolley
Sport Contact situations, a palm off and scrum in rugby, bench press

4 Pulling
Daily life Lifting an object with a pulley system
Sport Yachting, rowing, Tug-of-war

5 Bending
Daily life Parents picking up their kids/shopping basket, nurses, construction workers
Sport In golf when addressing the ball

6 Lunging (stooping down without bending the spine)
Daily life Fall prevention, traversing rough terrain
Sport Getting into position to tackle in hockey, goalkeeper blocking, fencing and badminton

7 Gait (walk; jog; sprints)
Daily life Getting around to school, to class, to work
Sport This forms the basis for all sports either directly during the play or training.

As well as the above, the circuits should also involve activities such as running, balancing and jumping. Teaching young people to handle their own body, as well as working the non-dominant limbs, is a must at this point in their development.

using circuits

The principles of circuit training should be taught at an early stage enabling athletes to develop sound technical mastery, strength and fitness base. I have used this type of circuit (outlined below), when first placing the teenagers I coach on a programme. The eight exercises shown are not the only ones I use, but I have found these to be a great conditioner, as well as preventing injury. In addition the core work illustrated develops the basic core strength required.

Sample circuit session

I have outlined some basic training here to develop a high level of fitness in youth players. The key thing to remember is that youngsters respond positively to short explosive work with plenty of recovery periods, and a lower level of aerobic work. Training youngsters within the Anaerobic Lactate energy systems is not appropriate for this age group.

Lunges (static)

Lunges are often done badly with common faults being the player's upper body leaning too far forward and the front knee travelling forward placing stress on the knee ligaments. The correct technique is to start with the square/right angles at the knee joint and lower the body vertically to the ground and then vertically up.

Sprint arms

Using weights as a resistance (this can be plastic bottles filled with water or sand according to the player's needs) the player stands with one foot ahead of the other, moving the arms in a sprinting manner. The weights are increased with improvement in strength.

Step runs

This is simply running up steps. If the players do 2 at a time, it assists in the driving movement required when running and requires knee pick up and use of the gluts.

Dips

Using a bench/chair or a large stadium step. The player places the hands behind them on the bench with the fingers facing forwards, the feet are kept well in front with loose straight legs. Ensuring only the arms are used, the player pushes up against the bench, lifting their whole body.

Step jumps

The starting and finishing position is a 90 degree leg squat position. The player leaps up two or three steps, driving the arms as part of the process. The 90 degree starting and finishing position ensures the large muscles (gluts, quads and erector spinae) are recruited. The spine must be flat (not rounded) throughout the movement.

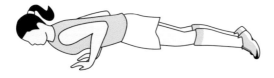

Press ups

Often done poorly because coaches teach only one method straight off the floor. Modify the movement if the player cannot execute this exercise with maintenance of neutral posture (maintaining a straight line from the ankle, through the ears and ensuring no articulation occurs at the waist or the neck, as shown). Simply ask the player to stand facing a solid wall with their feet around 80–100 cms from the wall, then execute the press up against the wall. If there is no articulation either from the waist or the neck, then this is appropriate to this player's ability. Progress until player can execute on the floor with no articulation.

Bulgarian Squat

Place one foot behind on a solid bench or step. The correct technique is to start with square/right angles in the back leg and lower the body vertically to the ground and then vertically up. Keep the arms crossed on the chest.

Sled runs

Using a purpose built sled or a car tyre attached by a rope to the athlete's waist, simply run the prescribed distance ensuring good basic running form is not compromised.

Circuit Training for Core Stability

The Plank and Side Plank

The player adopts the face down position shown in position 1 below, ensuring the neutral position is maintained throughout. When the body is in a neutral position, an imaginary line can be drawn from the ankle, through the hip to the ears.

The player then simply maintains this position for a specific duration. Then the player pushes into a press-up position and onto one arm with the body turned to the side for a side plank (position 2), then the other arm. Finally the player moves into position to hold a press-up.

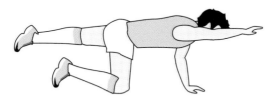

The Horse Stance

The player adopts the position shown ensuring the correct limb angles are adopted with the head in neutral. Slowly the player lifts the right arm and left leg to the positions shown and this is held for the required duration. Repeat on the opposite side.

Points to note:

1 Pull the belly button in towards the spine prior to the exercise.
2 Ensure the pelvis remains parallel to the ground throughout the movement.
3 The arm remains at 90 degrees to the shoulders as illustrated.

PRACTICE SESSION ORGANISATION

player empowerment

Teaching self-discipline is vital to a player's development. Players should be organised to assist the coach in setting out and clearing up all of the equipment. If this happens the players derive part ownership of the session, and have some input in the manner in which it is run. This relieves any time pressures and allows more time for practice. Developing a co-operative approach also assists preparation prior to competitions and assists in bonding the individuals within the team/squad.

equipment

Balls

Make sure as many are available as possible because time spent chasing loose or misfielded balls reduces time available for practice. Using 50–100 balls is not uncommon for practice nowadays. These can be purchased at a reasonable price.

For safety reasons ensure that all loose balls are removed from the practice areas and deposited in a conveniently located 'ball pool' area. This will be money well spent, but do ensure that if you start with 50 balls that is the number you finish with!

Goals

Real goals can be used in some training drills with extra goals being available at some venues nowadays.

Rebound boards are also useful as goals and are very mobile. Goalkeepers should always be fully kitted and even use extra padding during practice.

Markers

These come in the shape of:

- Cones – from small sizes to a 'motorway' size
- Domes – these are solid and half spherical in shape
- Discs – light and flimsy, these don't pose an injury risk if stood on but can blow away in the wind
- 'Witches' hats' – these are pointed and closed at the top.

Markers may be used for marking out the zones, setting up goals and pattern formers, with large cones being used as 'opponents' and as practice for lifting drills. In addition 2 m lengths of foam roll can also be used as opponents, but they tend to roll away in the wind.

Lattes

These are primarily deployed as tools for developing leg speed, but can also be used in other areas. For example, you can combine them with cones to build micro hurdles for lateral jump training.

Space

Drills can be set up anywhere on a pitch although care should be taken to ensure that where shooting or hitting is involved, they are done at a side or end line so that no one is behind the shooting area.

Some of the games drills are pitch direction orientated and can be run in specific areas of the pitch, but they can also be used across the pitch if only a half pitch is available (i.e. if the first and second eleven are training on the pitch at the same time).

Numbers can and will restrict some practices but, like all group-coaching, balances have to be struck. On a full pitch, up to five players is very easy – almost individual tuition with feeders; 5–12 players enables small group practices, and allows the possibility of removing an individual for corrective skills work; 12–20 players means that practice sessions will include queuing or built-in rest time. Above 20 players will certainly mean a great deal of practice management!

Pitch

The pitch diagram below shows that there are 10 areas that are readily available. Areas can be used on their own or combined – for example, using 8 and 9 to allow end line practice with a goal attempt; area 10 would allow a goal line practice feeding the ball to the end line and striker timing his run; area 7 at the other end could be GK practices; 11 and 12 may be used as extra goals.

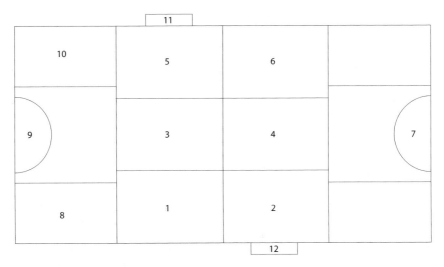

Figure 1 Sectioned pitch as a training area.

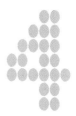

WARMING UP

Warming up for a match or training session is something that is often performed badly and ineffectively.

Although the advice in the following section follows specific scientific principles, it must be remembered that warm-ups are also of a highly personal nature. The player needs to make sure that they have completed enough of a warm-up to feel ready within themselves.

Why should you warm up?
The two main benefits of warming up are:

- Physical preparation
- Psychological preparation.

The two main goals of warming up are:

- to raise performance level
- to decrease risk of injury.

Physical preparation
- Raising the core muscle temperature
- Stretching/mobility
- Visual motor cues
- Sport specific (Functional)
- Engaging the central nervous system.

Psychological preparation
- Helps to reduce pre-competition nerves
- Players can use this time to mentally rehearse their role in the forthcoming competition
- A well organised team warm-up will look professional.

Phase 1 (0–10 minutes or the first third of the warm-up) Assemble the players at the side of the pitch. Throughout the warm-up the players will be working out and back across the width of the pitch. Start at a gentle pace by jogging to the far touchline and back. This is continuous, out and back across the pitch without stopping. Once the players have been jogging for 5–6 minutes teach them to perform the warm-up drills 1–11, mixing all of these movements in with the jogging for ten minutes.

NB: Drills 3, 4 and 5 should be started gradually, building the intensity as the warm-up progresses. Start with the players moving individually through the drill at their own intensity until a good speed is reached.

Phase 2 (10–20 minutes or the second third of the warm-up) On

reaching the sideline the players perform stretching. The format will be to stretch a muscle group, say the hamstrings, then go out to the far sideline and return and stretch another muscle, the quads, and so on. This method minimises core body temperature loss during stretching. Continue to deploy the variety of movement outlined in phase 1 as the players move out and back over the pitch.

Phase 3 (20–30 minutes or last third of the warm-up) Building up the

intensity is what this phase is all about. Drill 12 on page 26 is ideal for this purpose.

After this get the players to perform visual motor reaction work. In the same groups the players run towards the coach and as they do so must watch the coach. The coach then points his hand indicating the direction in which the players must move. The players must focus and react quickly to the coach's cues.

Purpose: Reverse jog (with left and right turn)

Practice set-up: Players should jog backwards, taking care not to collide with other players using the same space. On the coach's signal, players should reverse jog to their left or right.

drill 2

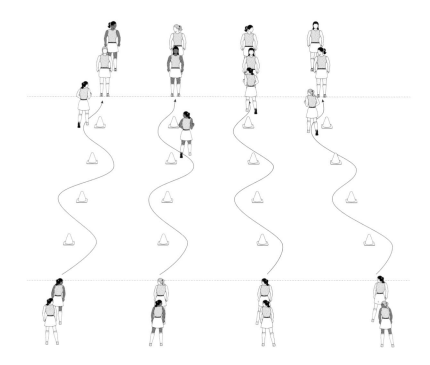

Purpose: Shuttle relays and sprint with slalom run; to develop pace, agility and competitiveness

Practice set-up: Split players up into teams of 4–6. Using the 25 m and 50 m lines, deploy half the team on the 25 m line and the remaining half on the 50 m line directly opposite their team mates. Use a bib as a 'baton', and on the whistle the race starts with the teams' first player sprinting and passing the bib to the second player, who sprints towards the third and so on until all players have run once each. The players perform a run through the cones as illustrated.

Equipment: Bibs and four markers per team

Tip: If one or two teams consistently dominate, rearrange the teams to ensure an even spread of talent across the teams.

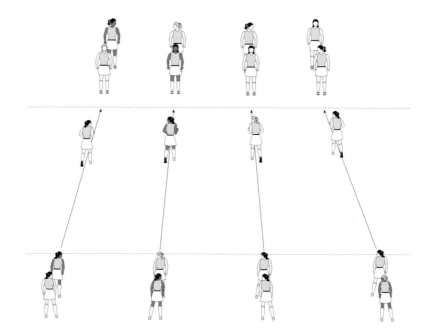

Purpose: Shuttle relays with straight sprint; to develop pace and competitiveness

Practice set-up: Split players up into teams of 4–6. Using the 25 m and 50 m lines, deploy half the team on the 25 m line and the remaining half on the 50 m line, directly opposite their team mates. Use a bib as a 'baton'. On the whistle the race starts with the teams' first player sprinting and passing the bib to the second player, who sprints towards the third and so on until all players have run once each.

Equipment: Bibs

Tip: If one or two teams consistently dominate, rearrange the teams to ensure an even spread of talent across the teams.

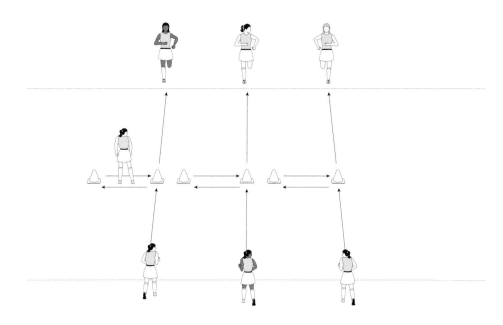

Purpose: T-Shuttle relays with slip step; to develop agility, pace and competitiveness

Practice set-up: Split players up into teams of 4–6. Using the 25 m and 50 m lines, deploy half the team on the 25 m line and the remaining half on the 50 m line directly opposite their team mates. Use a bib as a 'baton'. On the whistle the race starts with the teams' first players sprinting and passing the bib to the second player, who sprints towards the third and so on until all players have run once each.

The players should slip step from marker 1 to 2 then back to marker 1 then sprint as illustrated.

Equipment: Bibs and two markers per team

Tip: If one or two teams consistently dominate, rearrange the teams to ensure an even spread of talent across the teams.

Purpose: To develop agility, pace and competitiveness using a stick and ball

Practice set-up: This drill continues on from the athletic running and stretching and may be used entirely or in part depending on time and weather. As a lot of players may be on the move in a restricted area this must be coach controlled. Get the players to take the ball for a walk and a jog within the designated area. Tell them to dribble as they go, and change direction but be aware of other players around them and avoid collision. Coach to call when players should switch between running and jogging.

Equipment: Markers to indicate the area of play; each player will need a stick and ball

Tip: Players should be constantly reminded to look, to use their eyes to see space as well as other players and their movements even though they themselves are under pressure. This is needed in the match situation.

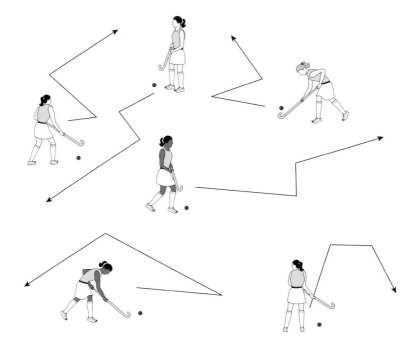

Purpose: To build on skill and pace using a stick and ball

Practice set-up: Using an area of 20 m by 20 m, get the players to change speed and pace – jog, run into space, jog again looking for another space or jog away from congestion.

Equipment: Markers to indicate the area of play; each player will need a stick and ball

Tip: Reduce the size of the working area as the players improve.

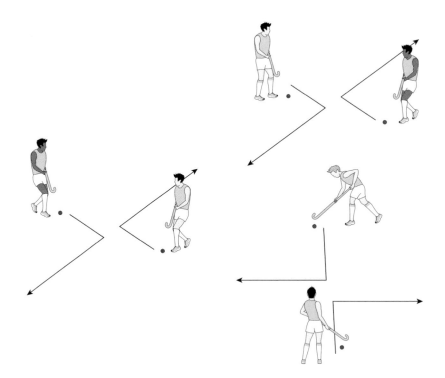

Purpose: To increase player understanding of spatial awareness and changing direction

Practice set-up: Players to move around a 20 m by 20 m area by jogging and running in the direction indicated by the coach. Every time one player approaches another, they should both change direction to their right. The coach should call 'stop' every so often, and on restarting the players should change direction to the left as they approach another player.

Equipment: Markers to indicate the area of play; each player will need a stick and ball

Purpose: To increase player awareness of moving within a restricted space and moving quickly away from opponents

Practice set-up: The same as in drill 7, but with the area reduced by one third. The players will still need to look for space to move into, but as each player dribbles they should try to tap the ball away from any other player they are close to while retaining their own. If a player's ball is knocked away, they should get it before coming back in to the game.

Equipment: Markers to indicate the area of play; each player will need a stick and ball

drill 9

Purpose: To develop vigilance

Practice set-up: All the players stand within a 20 m by 20 m area. All the players will have sticks and balls, apart from two or three players from whom the coach will have removed the balls – these players become a 'thief'. Their task is to obtain a ball, within the rules of hockey. When a 'thief' wins a ball they become a normal player. The player that has lost the ball now becomes the 'thief', and they must try to obtain any ball apart from the one that they have just lost. Thieves keep changing so players must keep watch for this and continually look for spaces to get into.

Equipment: Markers to indicate the area of play; each player will need a stick, and balls for all players except the 'thieves'

Progression: Increase the number of 'thieves' by withdrawing a ball every so often until the 'thieves' outnumber the normal players. Reduce the size of the working area as the players improve. This will require greater ball control, a greater number of tackles and increased vigilance.

drill 10

Purpose: To practise gaining and retaining possession of the ball

Practice set-up: All players divide into pairs within a 20 m by 20 m area. Each pair has one ball, and they stand facing each other, one stick length away from the ball with their stick against their right foot. When the coach shouts 'go' they both try to get possession of the ball. When the coach shouts 'stop' the winner is the player in possession. The coach should vary the time between the 'go' and 'stop' commands to between one and ten seconds. Each pair should play best of three, before the winner keeps the ball and stands still, and the loser moves on to another opponent with a ball.

Equipment: Markers to indicate the area of play; stick for each player, and a ball for every pair

A   B

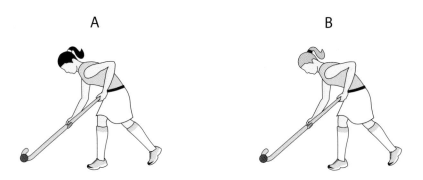

Purpose: To practise marking an opponent in play and to improve skills and reactions

Practice set-up: All players divide into pairs within the marked area. They have a ball each, and player B stands two metres behind player A. When the coach shouts 'go', A moves off by dribbling in any direction, changing as frequently as they want to. The aim of player A will be to lose player B; the aim of player B will be to remain two metres behind A at all times. After a certain amount of time, the players can swap roles.

Equipment: Markers to indicate the area of play; each player will need a stick and ball

Progression: Coach can develop this drill by calling 'change'. When the players hear this, they must immediately swap roles, and the player leading becomes the player chasing. This mimics ball possession being lost by the lead team, and teaches players to quickly switch from attacking to defending.

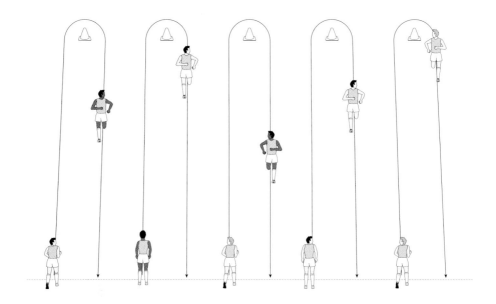

Purpose: To prepare mentally and physically for full running action

Practice set-up: Divide the players into groups of three or four and line them up on the sideline. On the coach's signal the players accelerate out to a marker placed at around 30 m. The coach must stress the importance of gradually building up each subsequent run until full effort is realised on the last two runs. The players perform six runs of gradually increasing intensity with the last two runs being done at flat out intensity.

Equipment: A cone for each team to mark the 30 m mark

MOVEMENT SKILLS

The drills in this chapter teach the players a variety of skills that will improve their motor fitness. This will enable the player to possess a far greater level of motor skill, motor control and coordination. These drills stress the ability to achieve multi-direction change rapidly, stoop low, and recover and react quickly to a visual stimulus.

All these opponents. I'm out of here!! Ester Termenes (Spain) threads through and runs away from three German defenders.

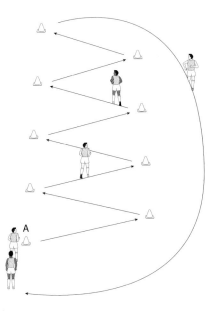

Purpose: To teach the players to change direction smoothly and improve balance

Practice set up: Assemble the players at point A, and set up the cones in a zigzag pattern at intervals of 5 m. On the whistle the first player starts to run to each marker, stepping off right leg when changing direction to the left; stepping off the left leg when changing direction to the right. When the first player reaches the mid point the next player starts. The players then walk back to point A.

Equipment: Nine markers

Tip: Start the players off initially by jogging through the pattern required, and building up speed as their confidence grows. Aim for the players to run smoothly throughout the movement eliminating any long steps and clumsy movements.

drill 14

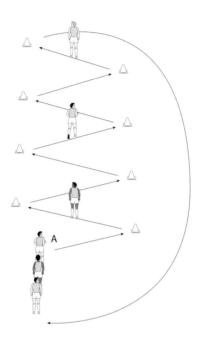

Purpose: To teach the players to change direction smoothly and improve balance

Practice set-up: Assemble the players at point A, and set up the cones in a zigzag pattern at intervals of 5 m. On the whistle the first player runs to the first marker, then slip steps left to the second, runs to the third, then slip steps left to the fourth and so on until the last marker. When the first player reaches the mid point the next player starts. The players then walk back to point A.

Equipment: Eight markers

Purpose: To develop the ability to check whilst running forwards, to then rapidly change and reverse run

Practice set up: Set out the markers as illustrated at a spacing of anything between 3 and 5 m. The players start at marker number 1, sprint to marker 3 and reverse jog to marker 2. On reaching marker 2 the player sprints to marker 4. This is repeated in this manner until marker 6 is reached, then the player drops back to marker 5 then sprints past marker 6. Three to four players can use each station at one time provided they use a staggered start.

Equipment: Six markers

drill 16

Purpose: To develop speed and agility

Practice set-up: Players to stand in a line. Set out the first two markers 10 m apart and the remaining markers at 1.5–3 m intervals. On the start signal, the player sprints through the course as illustrated. The players must aim to move through the markers fluently deploying a balanced change of direction through the markers.

Equipment: Eight markers

Progression: On reaching the last marker the player turns around and heads back down the same route, completing two laps. He will then tap the next player in line, and they will complete the same run.

Purpose: To develop speed, fast feet and agility

Practice set-up: Set out the markers at 1 m intervals. On the start signal the first player works his way through the course as illustrated. The players must aim to move through the markers fluently deploying a balanced change of direction and deploying fast feet through the markers.

Equipment: Ten to twelve markers

drill 18

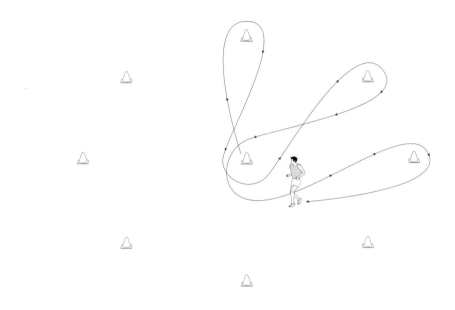

Purpose: To develop agility and turning ability

Practice set-up: Set out the markers in a circle, making either a four- or eight-legged spider. The players take it in turns to run the course, starting and finishing at the centre marker. On the start signal the first player runs around all the markers via the centre marker, turning left at the centre marker and right at the outer markers. Encourage players to perform a fancy turn at the outer markers.

Equipment: Seven to nine markers

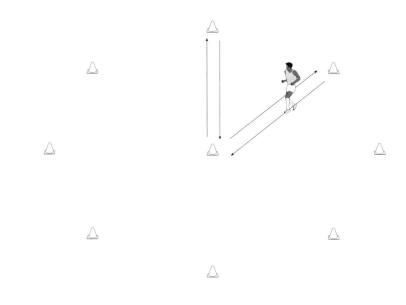

Purpose: To develop agility, reverse movement and turning ability

Practice set-up: Set out the markers in a circle, making either a six or eight-legged spider. The players take it in turns to run the course, starting and finishing at the centre marker. On the start signal the first player runs to an outer marker then reverse runs back to the centre marker. The player then runs to the next outer marker. This is continued until all markers have been visited.

Equipment: Seven to nine markers

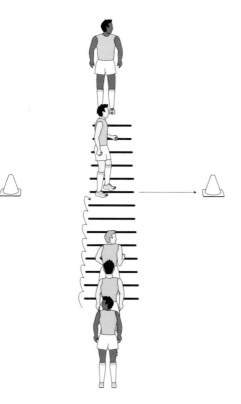

Purpose: To develop visual motor cues

Practice set-up: The lattes are laid on the ground at 1 m intervals, with 2 markers placed 3–5 m out to the sides. The players stand in a line, and when the coach shouts 'go' the first player starts running 'fast feet' down the lattes. The coach then shouts 'left' or 'right' at which point the player must react quickly to the command and run to the nearest marker, touch it, then return to the place that they left the course and resume running. Depending on when the coach shouts and how fast the player reacts, the athlete will be required to vary their angles.

Equipment: Two markers, 10–20 lattes (sticks)

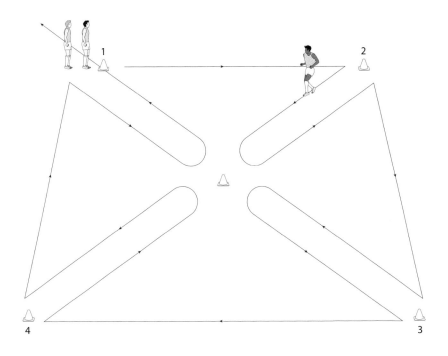

Purpose: To develop agility and fast foot work; to improve the player's ability to change direction on tight angles in a relatively tight space and over a relatively long intense period of time

Practice set-up: Set up the markers as illustrated with the four markers forming a 10 m square. On the start signal, the player proceeds around the route as indicated. On reaching the centre marker the player simply touches it before moving to the outer markers. One full lap is completed when the player touches the centre marker for the last time before running back to marker 1. The next player starts as soon as the player in front returns to marker 2 from the centre marker.

Equipment: Six markers

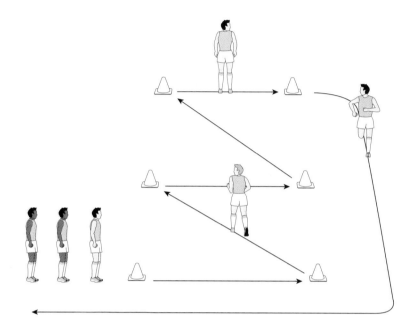

Purpose: To develop speed and agility

Practice set-up: Set out the markers as indicated at around 5 m in width and 10 m in length. The players stand in a line at marker 1, and on the start signal the first player slip steps to marker 2, sprints to marker 3, slip steps to marker 4, sprints to marker 5 and so on. This movement is maintained until the last marker is reached where the player then jogs back to the start point. Once the first player reaches the mid point the second player can go.

Equipment: Six markers

Purpose: To train the capacity of the player to react to a visual stimulus; to improve change of direction and agility

Practice set up: The players divide into pairs. Set out two rows of three markers at 5 m apart. The players start at the centre marker and one is elected to be 'it'. This player leads while the other one tries to follow his movements as closely as possible, and 'mirror' them exactly. Run this session for a set amount of time, for example 30 seconds, before the players exchange being 'it'. It will then be the turn of the next pair in line.

Equipment: Six markers

Purpose: To train the capacity of the player to react to a visual stimulus, change of direction and agility

Practice set-up: The players divide into pairs. Set out three markers at 5 m apart. The first pair start at the centre and one is elected to be 'it'. This player leads while the other one tries to follow his movements as closely as possible, and 'mirror' them exactly. Run this session for a set amount of time, for example 30 seconds, before another player is elected to be 'it'. It will then be the turn of the next pair in line. This time the players can work with more depth, increasing the possibilities of varying the movement patterns.

Equipment: Three markers

Over the Hurdle – the ball first and then the foot. Looks like a reverse hit for goal coming up from Prabhjoth Singh of India.

STICK AND BALL SKILLS

The drills in this section will need to be adapted by the coach to match the abilities of the players that they are working with at the time. They may have to simplify what they already consider a simple drill in order to allow the player to succeed, without losing sight of the objective of the drill.

Coaches should be working to actively improve poor technique as the player performs, or as soon as the player completes the drill. Players should be encouraged to go through a drill without the ball to get the footwork correct and the pattern of the drill before putting themselves through the stick and ball routine.

Picking up the ball cleanly is a vital part of stick and ball work as it allows a player to move into the next phase easily and earlier than if they have to readjust in a second touch. The ball comes from all directions and players must be able to take this standing still or on the move, and off the right or left foot. Once this is mastered the player is in control of the ball and all the other skills of hockey are made easier.

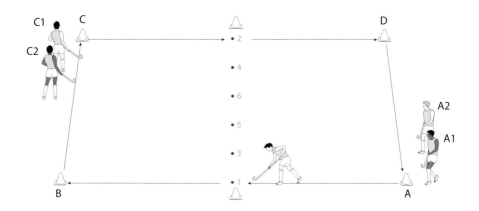

Purpose: To develop confidence in picking up the ball on the run, off either foot with no break in the stride pattern

Practice set-up: The markers are placed in two lines 10 m apart, forming a rectangular grid. Six balls are placed in a line in the centre, at 1 m intervals. Each grid has three players assigned to it, and they line up at marker A, A1 and A2. The player at A takes three strides to the first marker, starting with the right foot, and picking up ball 1 on the third stride (also on right foot). Keeping the same stride pattern the player stops the ball at marker B, and jogs to marker C. The player then runs towards marker D, this time starting on the left foot, and as before, collecting ball 2 on the third stride (also on the left foot). The player stops the ball at D and jogs back to A.

   When the first player has reached marker C1 the second player can go, following the same pattern and collecting balls 3 and 4. When the second player has reached marker C1 the third player can go, collecting balls 5 and 6. Replace the balls and repeat.

Equipment: Sticks for all players; six balls and six markers

Tip: Ensure that this drill is completed with straight continuous running, with no break in the stride pattern.

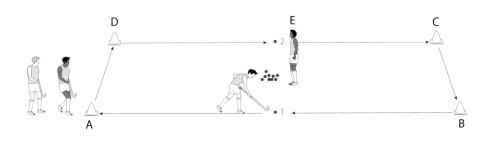

Purpose: To develop confidence in picking up the ball on the run, off either foot with no break in the stride pattern

Practice set-up: Four markers are placed as shown above, to create a rectangular grid ABCD with a ball at positions 1 and 2 (3 metres apart). Each grid has 4 players assigned to it. Three players start at marker A. One player stands between balls 1 and 2 with a bin of balls. The first player takes three strides from marker A, starting with the right foot and picking up ball 1 on the third stride (also on the right foot). Keeping the same stride pattern throughout the player stops the ball at marker B. The player then moves to marker C and runs back, starting on the left foot, to marker D, picking up the ball number 2 (also on the left foot).

When a ball is removed it is replaced by a ball from the bin by the player in the centre. The next player runs and picks up the ball and so it continues. Change the centre player every 20 balls.

Equipment: Sticks for all players; bin of balls and four markers

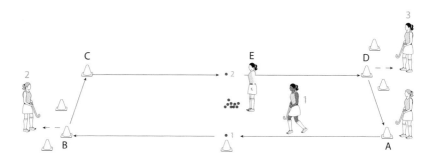

Purpose: To develop confidence in passing the ball accurately on the run, off either foot with continuous stride pattern; develop skills when moving to collect a pass

Practice set-up: Four markers create a rectangular grid ABCD, while another four markers are used as target posts for the pass. Two balls are placed in a line 2 m apart. Each grid has five players assigned to it, two at marker A, one positioned behind the first target post by B and one positioned behind the last target post by D. The last player is positioned at E between balls 1 and 2 with a bin of balls.

The first player at A takes three strides to the first ball, starting with the right foot, and picking up ball 1 on the third stride (also on right foot). Keeping the same stride pattern they go forwards with the ball towards B and push the ball to the player 2 when their right foot strikes the ground. Player 2 moves into the target to collect the pass, and stops the ball. Player 1 continues to jog to marker C and then runs towards D, this time starting on the left foot and collecting ball 2 on the third stride (also on the left foot). Keeping the same stride pattern player 1 pushes the ball to player 3 when their left foot strikes the ground. Player 3 moves into the target to collect the pass, and stops the ball. Player 1 jogs back to A. The player at E replaces a removed ball and the next player goes from A. Then all the players swap positions until each player has had an opportunity to play at each post. Rotate players after 20 pickups.

Equipment: Sticks for all players; six balls and eight markers

drill 28

Purpose: To gain confidence in passing the ball accurately on the run, off either foot with a continuous stride pattern; develop skills when moving to collect a pass

Practice set-up: Four markers create a thin rectangular grid, while another four markers are used as target posts for the pass. Six balls are placed in a line 10 cm apart, except in the middle where the gap is 2 m. Each grid has three players assigned to it, one at marker A, one positioned behind the first target post by B and one positioned behind the last target post by D.

The player at A takes three strides to the first ball, starting with the right foot, and picking up ball 1 on the third stride (also on right foot). Keeping the same stride pattern they go forwards with the ball towards B and push the ball to the player 2 when their right foot strikes the ground. Player 2 moves into the target to collect the pass, and stops the ball. Player 1 turns left and runs towards marker D, this time starting on the left foot and collecting ball 2 on the third stride (also on the left foot). Keeping the same stride pattern player 1 pushes the ball to player 3 when their left foot strikes the ground. Player 3 moves into the target to collect the pass, and stops the ball. Player 1 runs back to A and repeats for balls 3–6, then all the players swap positions until each player has had an opportunity to play at each post.

Equipment: Sticks for each player; six balls and eight markers

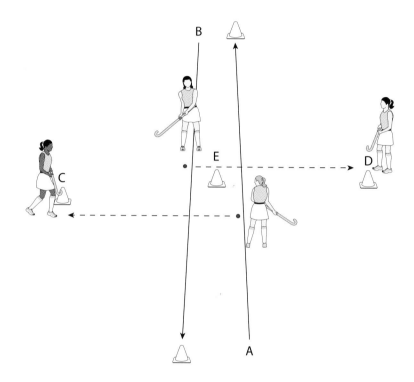

Purpose: To pass the ball to the left and right on the run

Practice set-up: Each grid has four players assigned to it, with a player at markers A, B, C and D. Another marker is placed in the centre of the grid at E. The players at A and B have a ball each, and they run towards each other, passing either side of marker E. Just before they reach marker E, they both pass to their left to the players at C and D, who move forwards to collect the pass. C and D then run towards each other, passing either side of marker E. Just before they reach marker E, they both pass to their left to A and B. Play continues in this manner. All players should run to the right of the marker for safety.

Equipment: Sticks for each player; two balls and five markers

Tip: To pass right, run the same pattern but, before marker E, turn the stick to pass right. Player A will pass to D and player B to C.

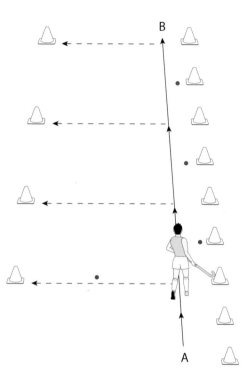

Purpose: To pick up a ball and pass it to the left and right on the run

Practice set-up: One player makes a straight run forwards, starting at marker A. Picking up a ball at the first marker, they pass it to their left at the next marker, and continue down the line with pick up at one marker and pass at the next.

Equipment: Two markers for start and finish; four markers for the passes; eight markers for the run; four balls

Progression: (a) Pick up at marker 1, drive forwards to marker 2, check and drag back to marker 1, before driving forwards to pass at marker 2. Repeat down the line; (b) Use eight markers and place closer together; (c) Pass on reverse stick to the right; (d) Pass alternately first ball to the left and the second on the reverse to the right.

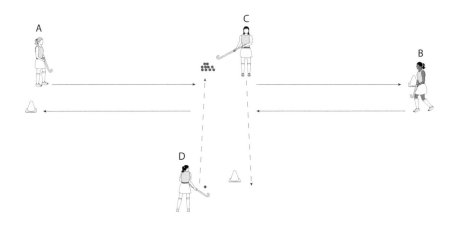

Purpose: Gaining confidence in picking up a moving ball while on the move, and running with it under control; collecting a pass, making a pass while stationary and timing a pass to a running player

Practice set-up: Four players are assigned to each grid. Two markers are positioned 20 m apart, with player A and B positioned at each one. Players C and D are positioned halfway between the markers at 5 m apart. Player C has a pool of 10 balls at his feet. C and D inter-pass a ball to each other. A runs towards the gap and picks up the ball that is being passed between C and D and runs on towards B with the ball.

  C and D continue to pass another ball from the ball pool, and B makes his run, collecting the ball in the same way as A. Play continues until all 10 runs have been made. Then A and B swap places with C and D and play is repeated.

Equipment: Sticks for each player; 10 balls and two markers

Progression: Add three markers after the pick up point for the player to weave through; widen the gap between C and D to increase the need for accuracy and also improve player timing of a pass to a running player.

DRIBBLING UNDER CONTROL

Dribbling with the ball on the move is difficult enough, but when you add in opponents chasing, the constraints of the side and end lines, and the need to watch and think about passing and shooting, life on the pitch can become very stressful. Good dribbling practice can assist players to keep cool, calm and controlled when the going gets tough. It will allow them to get clear of traffic on the pitch and make strong and effective passes and shots.

Stephen Edwards (New Zealand) thinks he is away and clear but Aussies do not give up that easily and the chase is on.

Purpose: Gaining confidence when running fast in possession of the ball; keeping the ball under control

Practice set-up: Three players are assigned to each grid, each with their own ball. Player 1 starts at A, player 2 waits at marker B, and player 3 waits behind player 1. Player 1 drives forwards fast with the ball for 10 m to marker B. Player 1 stops the ball dead at marker B, slows down and turns back around to wait at the marker. Player 2 then takes off with their ball to marker A where they stop the ball dead, and turn back around to wait at the marker. This triggers player 3 to start off with their ball to marker B and so on.

Equipment: Sticks for each player; three balls and two markers

Progression: Introduce two additional markers between A and B. Players start at A, running fast to the first marker, and then slowing to the second, before accelerating onto B. This mimics the acceleration and deceleration in many hockey matches.

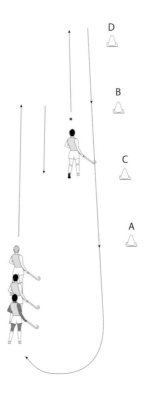

Purpose: Gaining confidence in running fast in possession, with the ball under control and including a change of direction

Practice set-up: Four players are assigned to each grid. Four markers are placed in a line at intervals of 5 m. Players line up, with the first player in line with marker A. The first player drives their ball 10 m forwards to marker B, then pulls the ball back 5 m to marker C before driving forwards another 10 m to marker D. Player one then pulls the ball back 5 m to marker B, before running fast forwards to marker D, and joining the back of the line.

When the first player reaches marker D the second player starts the same process and the drill cycle continues.

Equipment: Sticks and balls for each player; four markers

Progression: Increase the number of markers to six, working on the same basis of 10 m forwards and 5 m back.

Purpose: To develop confidence and control when running with the ball through 'traffic'

Practice set-up: Three to four players are assigned to each grid. The four markers are placed in a line at intervals of 1 m. The players line up at point A to the left of the markers. The first player runs straight up and down to the left of the markers, while dribbling the ball forwards interweaving between the markers. The player does not interweave, just the ball. Players should use the 'Indian dribble' of stick over the ball – the ball should be kept on or outside the player's right foot on the way out, and on or outside the player's left foot on the way back. When the first player returns then the second player can go, and so on.

Equipment: A stick and ball for each player; four markers

Progression: Increase the number of markers to eight, and work on the same basis; slightly offset every odd number marker (a quarter of a metre or less) to the right to demand extra body and ball movement from the players; try the dribble with the stick behind the ball ('English dribble').

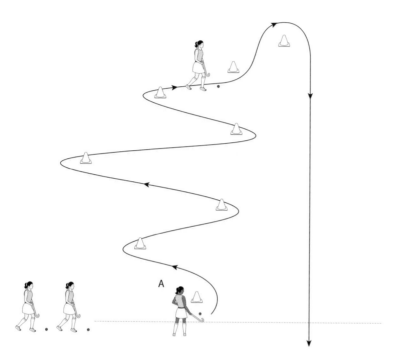

A

Purpose: To develop confidence and control when running with the ball through 'traffic'

Practice set-up: Three to four players are assigned to each grid. Eight markers are set out at varying intervals. Players line up at A, and the first player starts by dribbling forwards interweaving between markers, rounding the end marker and returning to the start. When the first player returns the next player goes. Players should use the 'Indian dribble' with the stick over the ball, and their feet must go round the markers as well as the ball.

Equipment: A stick and ball for each player; eight markers

Progression: Where you have set up more than one grid, have races. The first team with all their members back at the start after completing one lap of the course each wins.

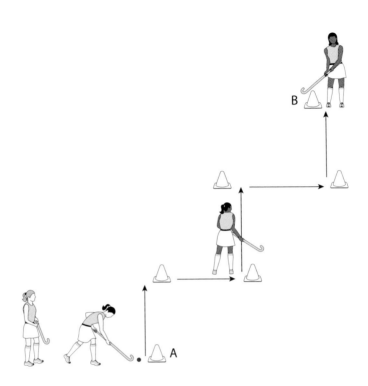

Purpose: To develop confidence and control when running with the ball and changing direction

Practice set-up: Three to four players are assigned to each grid. Place the six markers in a 'step' formation, at intervals of 3 m up and 3 m across. Two players start at marker A, and the other one at marker B. The first player drives the ball forwards to the first marker, slides (or slip steps) across to the next marker then drives forwards again and so on. When they have reached the top of the 'steps', the second player stationed at marker B starts making their way down in the same manner. When they reach the bottom, it is the turn of player 3. The play should continue in this way until all players have had a chance to go up and down the 'steps'.

Equipment: A stick and ball for each player; six markers

Progression: Increase the number of markers to eight, and work on the same basis; increase the distance between markers to 5 m; introduce a race between different teams.

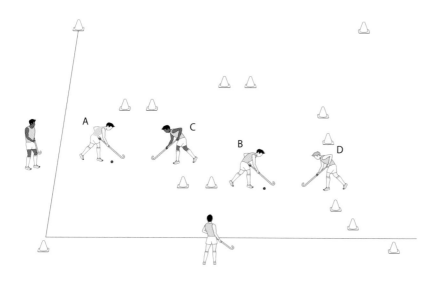

Purpose: To practice dribbling under control and retaining possession

Practice set-up: Place four corner markers to mark the designated area of play, approximately 20 m by 20 m; within this area place 10 markers in pairs as goals at various angles. Six players are assigned to each grid; two pairs start within the area with a ball between them, and two players wait on the sidelines on 'standby'. Players A and B start with the ball. They can change direction and attempt to run the ball through various goals and retain possession. If their partner wins possession away from them they have to leave the pitch to be replaced by the standby player. The game continues on in the same manner.

Equipment: A stick for each player and one ball for each pair; 14 markers

Progression: Possession player can pass to 'stand by' player who can return the pass.

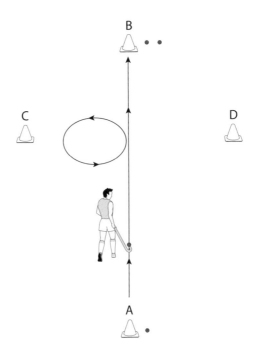

Purpose: To fool an opponent with a movement of the stick (dummy pass)

Practice set-up: One player makes a straight run forwards, starting at marker A towards marker B. When they are level with marker C wave the stick ('magic wand') over and round the front of the ball in an anti-clockwise direction. Believe you are going to pass the ball left but miss the ball which rolls merrily on in a straight line for you pick up and carry on to stop at B.

 Pick up another ball and head back to A repeating the dummy pass to D.

Equipment: Two markers for start and finish; two markers for the dummy pass; four balls

Progression: (a) Repeat for the reverse stick dummy. This time just go clockwise round the ball. (b) Do a dummy then pass on the next stride to C.

LIFTING AND COLLECTING THE BALL IN THE AIR

As defences become ever tighter and more compact, and defenders gain the ability to stretch and reach low with the stick to cover ground, it has become more and more necessary for players to learn how to lift the ball. This means that picking up the ball on the volley as well as on the bounce is needed by both attackers receiving passes, and by defenders intercepting.

Initially, lifting can be a problem for young players as they try too hard and become too tense. However they soon get the feeling for the action, and realise that a lot of strength is not required. Gradually they will find that they can fly the ball long distances but although this can look spectacular and is sometimes necessary to clear the ball away from defence, it is the low short lifts that are the most effective and are needed most often. The criterion here is danger if the lift is too near to other players and also on the landing where the receiver needs space to receive the ball.

Emma Clarke (Ireland) thinks 'In the air – I don't care. It is still my ball'. Good low right hand position on the stick.

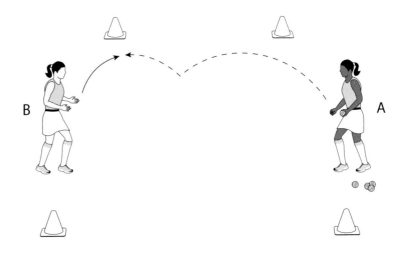

Purpose: To give the attacker the confidence to lift the ball over a defender's stick or goalkeeper's foot; to give the defender the confidence to collect a bouncing ball

Practice set-up: Four markers set out a square 3 m x 3 m. Players work in pairs within each square, with Player A having a pool of five tennis balls. Player A throws (flies) the first ball underarm across the channel (gap). Player B collects by catching the ball after the first bounce. Player A can alternate the direction and speed at which they throw the ball to allow player B to run forwards, backwards, slide sideways and change direction, but the ball must stay within the marked area.

When all five balls have been fed to player B, play reverses and player B feeds them back to player A in the same manner so both players have the opportunity to get used to the line of flight and bounce.

Equipment: Four markers; five tennis balls

Progression: Player A can move on to using a hockey ball, and player B can move on to using a stick to collect the ball.

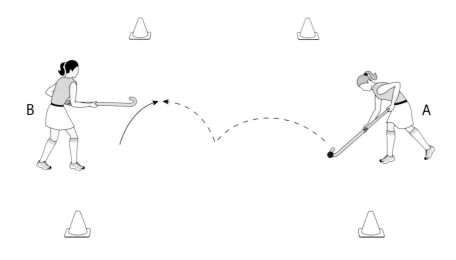

Purpose: To develop the confidence of the attacker to lift the ball over a defender's stick or goalkeeper's foot; to develop the confidence of the defender when collecting a bouncing ball

Practice set-up: Four markers set out a square 3 m x 3 m, and players work in pairs within each square. Player A flies the ball across the channel using their stick. Player B collects the ball with their stick after the first bounce, getting the ball to their right (front stick).

Player A can alternate the direction and speed at which they fly the ball to allow player B to run forwards, backwards, slide sideways and change direction, but the ball must stay within the marked area. B then passes the ball by ferry (flat pass) back to A across the channel. Once player A has made five passes, play reverses.

Equipment: A stick for each player and a ball for each pair; four markers

Progression: Make the channel wider by placing the markers at 5 m x 5 m.

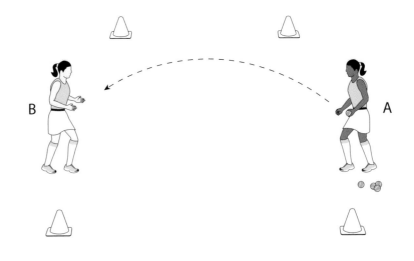

Purpose: To give the defender the confidence to collect a ball on the volley

Practice set-up: Four markers set out to create a square 3 m x 3 m. Players work in pairs within each square, with Player A having a pool of five tennis balls. Player A flies the first tennis ball underarm across the channel, and player B collects the ball by catching it on the volley (before it hits the ground). The most comfortable height to catch the ball is between waist and knee. Player A can alternate the direction and speed at which they throw the ball to allow player B to run forwards, backwards, slide sideways and change direction, but the ball must stay within the marked area.

When all five balls have been fed to player B, play reverses and player B feeds them back to player A in the same manner so both players have the opportunity to get used to the line of flight.

Equipment: Four markers and five tennis balls; for the progression you will need a stick for each pair and five hockey balls

Purpose: To give the defender the confidence to collect a ball on the volley; to give the attacker the confidence to fly the ball over a defender's stick or goalkeeper's foot and into space for a pass

Practice set-up: Four markers set out a square 3 m x 3 m, and players work in pairs within each square. Player A flies the ball across the channel using their stick. Player B collects the ball with their stick on the volley, getting the ball to their right (front stick).

Player A can alternate the direction and speed at which they fly the ball to allow player B to run forwards, backwards, slide sideways and change direction, but the ball must stay within the marked area. B then passes the ball by ferry (flat pass) back to A across the channel. Once player A has made five passes, play reverses.

Equipment: A stick for each player and a ball for each pair; four markers

Progression: Make the channel wider by placing the markers at 5 m x 5 m.

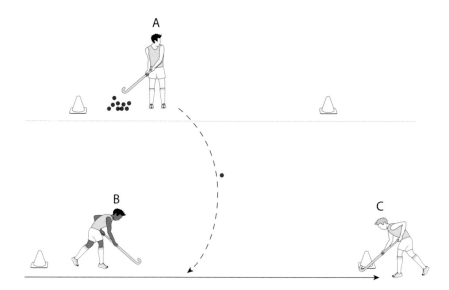

Purpose: To give the defender the confidence to collect a ball on the bounce from the right and left while on the move; to give the attacker the confidence to fly the ball over a defender's stick, goalkeeper's foot or into space for a pass

Practice set-up: Four markers are set out to create a rectangular grid, 8 m wide x 3 m deep. Three players are assigned to each grid, and player A starts with a pool of 10 balls. Player A flies the ball forwards over the channel, aiming for a point halfway between players B and C. Player B runs towards the ball, collecting it as it bounces and keeping the movement steady as he continues on towards player C. Player C then runs towards the next ball that player A flies, collecting it in the same manner. Once player A has passed all 10 balls forwards, players rotate positions and repeat until each player has had a chance to play at each post.

Equipment: A stick for each player and 10 balls; four markers

Progression: Make the channel slightly wider; try for a continuous stride pattern on the pick up.

drill 44

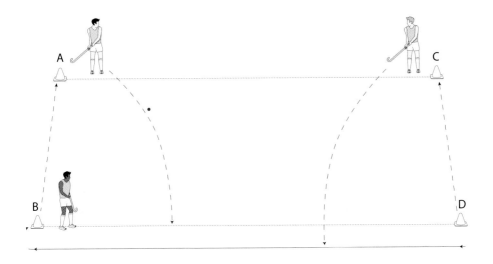

Purpose: To give players the confidence to collect a ball on the bounce from right and left while on the move; to give players the confidence to fly the ball over an opponent's stick, goalkeeper's foot or into space for a pass

Practice set-up: Four markers are set out to create a rectangular grid, 8 m wide x 3 m deep. Three players are assigned to each grid. Player A starts with the ball, and flies the ball forwards ahead of player B. Player B runs forwards to collect the ball on the bounce and moves forwards with it before ferrying the ball to player C. Player C collects the ball and flies it back to player B who collects it while running back to the start, and finishes by ferrying it back to player A. Continue in this manner until player A has made six passes. Players then rotate positions and repeat until each has had a chance to play at each post.

Equipment: A stick for each player and one ball per station; four markers

drill 45

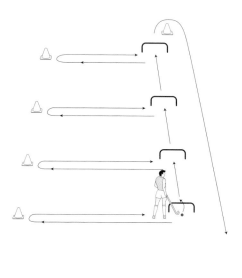

Purpose: To practise lifting the ball on the move over an opponent's stick or a goalkeeper's foot

Practice set-up: Players start at marker A. With their ball, the first player runs straight towards the first hurdle, and then slip steps sideways to the marker placed 3 m to the left. They then slip step sideways back to the hurdle, and lift the ball over the hurdle. They complete the other hurdles in exactly the same manner, before returning to the start. Once the first player has reached the second hurdle, the next player in line can start, and so on.

Equipment: A stick and ball for each player; six markers and four stick bags or mini hurdles

Progression: Place another line of markers 3 m to the right. The player slip steps right to the markers, then returns left to use a reverse lift over the hurdle. Some players find this easier than the front stick lift.

CHANGING DIRECTION

In a fast-moving and dynamic hockey match it is essential for players to be able to change direction quickly and with a great deal of accuracy. A player can achieve this by using the correct body and foot movements, and the earlier running drills provide a very sound base on which to build. The ability to change direction well will allow the player the freedom to move around and still be balanced and in control.

Oops. No way through or over this guy. Better try another route. Good weight over the ball and stick position by Carlos Nevado (Germany) against Belgium.

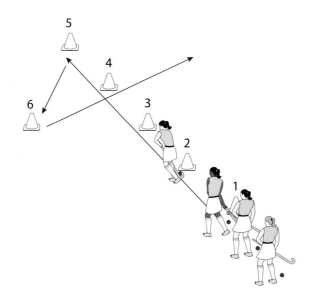

Purpose: To develop footwork skills and learn to change direction while moving with the ball; to allow players to develop defensive footwork

Practice set-up: Six markers are set out as indicated, approximately one stride apart. The players start at marker 1 with their left foot forwards. The first player sets off in a straight line with the ball, reaching the next marker with each stride. By marker 5, the player will be on their left foot, where they check the ball and step back to marker 6 with their right foot, at the same time dragging the ball back past their right foot. They then drive away on their front stick past marker 4 and return to the start. When the first player has completed the course the second player goes, and so on.

Equipment: A stick and ball for each player; six markers

Progression: Add an accurate pass to a target after the drive.

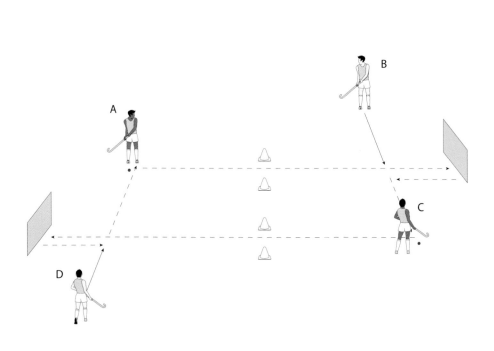

Purpose: To encourage players to make accurate flat sweeping hits, either passing from the back line to strikers and midfield or around the back line

Practice set-up: Four players are assigned to each grid. Use a side and end area line for this drill if possible, making the area of play 15 m long and 6 m wide. Four markers are placed as indicated, approximately halfway between the players and the rebound boards. Player A makes a sweeping pass through the first pair of markers towards the rebound board. Player B collects the ball on the rebound from the board, and passes it left to player C. Player C collects, and then makes a sweeping pass through the next pair of markers towards the second rebound board. Player D collects the ball on the rebound from the board, and passes back to player A.

Equipment: A stick for each player; four markers and two rebound boards; one ball

Progression: Add a player to the grid so there are two at the starting point A. Each player follows the ball to the next station. All then get practice of both pick up and pass.

drill 48

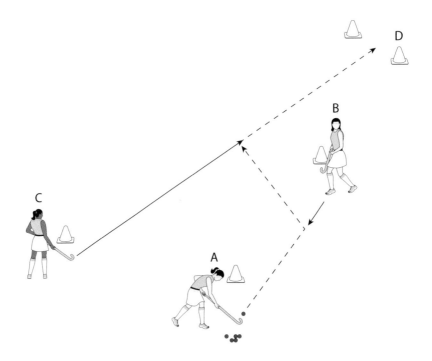

Purpose: To learn how to deflect a pass into the path of another player to allow a goal scoring opportunity

Practice set-up: Three players are assigned to each grid, with a player at markers A, B and C as shown. Two markers are placed at D to create a goal. Player A starts with a pool of six balls, and passes the first ball towards the player B. Player B moves to collect the ball, and deflects the pass off a low flat stick into the path of player C. Player C moves forwards to collect the ball, and shoots between the markers at D. This pattern is then repeated with the next ball in the pool. When all the balls have been used the players can rotate positions and repeat until each has had a chance to play at each post.

Equipment: A stick for each player; five markers and six balls

Progression: Use five players, with two at marker B and two at marker C. Have a bin of balls at A for continuous practice.

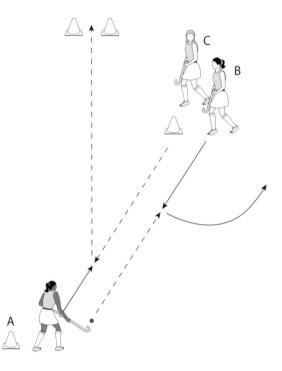

Purpose: To develop passing between players while on the move; to teach players to react quickly to a goal scoring opportunity

Practice set-up: Three players are assigned to each grid. Four markers are set out as indicated, with two markers creating a goal, and two markers to indicate player starting positions. Players A and B work as a pair, with player C initially marking player B. Player A moves forwards and passes the ball to player B. Player B receives the pass, and returns it to A. The aim of player B is to make things difficult for player C by moving away from C to the right into a space to receive the next pass. If player C follows player B, then player A should take the opportunity to drive the ball through the space created towards the goal. If player C moves in to mark player A, then A needs to quickly pass the ball to player B who should have the space to drive the ball forwards to the goal.

Equipment: A stick for each player; one ball and four markers

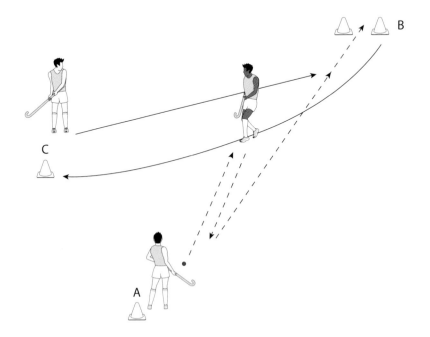

Purpose: To develop passing skills while on the move and to create space and then use it

Practice set-up: Three players are assigned to each grid. Four markers are set out as shown to indicate player starting positions. Player A starts with possession of the ball, and passes it to player B who is moving forwards to collect it. Player B receives the pass, and returns it to A before continuing on to marker C. The player at C runs towards the space created at marker B, picking up the pass from A and scoring a goal. Player B continues alongside player C, with player A supporting from behind.

Equipment: A stick for each player; one ball and four markers

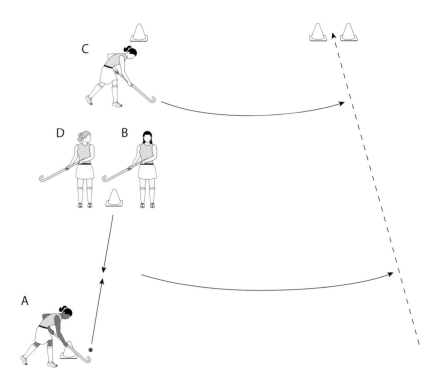

Purpose: Using a forward to help other players gain an opportunity to score; to change direction when under pressure

Practice set-up: Four players are assigned to each grid. Three markers are set out as shown to indicate player starting positions. Two markers are placed to create a goal. Player A starts with possession of the ball, and passes it to player B who is moving forwards to collect it, with player D marking. Player B takes the pass and moves off to attack right in order to move into a space to pass to player C. Player C makes a later run to collect the ball, and B then continues his run to support C in attack with the aim of scoring a goal at the earliest opportunity. After a goal has been scored players can rotate positions and repeat the same movement.

Equipment: A stick for each player; one ball and five markers

MARKING AND LOSING A MARKER

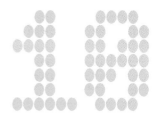

Mirror practices help to ensure that a player learns to watch the actions of their opponent, and this in turn will allow them to react earlier to danger than might otherwise be the case. This can lead to winning the ball by interception, which is essential in the modern game.

Ready? Then here we come. French defence pour out to defend a short corner against Ireland. Where would you put the ball if you were the shooter?

Purpose: To improve player vision and reaction in attack and defence

Practice set-up: Two markers are positioned 10 m apart, using a pitch line. Players work in pairs, facing each other across this line. Player A has possession of the ball, and sidesteps left and right at varying speeds with as many stops and starts as they want. Player B attempts to stay opposite player A at all times. Players should take it in turns to be the leader.

Equipment: A stick for each player and a ball for each pair; two markers

Progression: Give both players a ball, and repeat as above; A can attempt to get the ball over the line and back again before B can touch it.

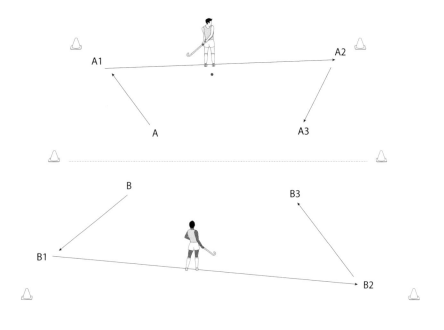

Purpose: To improve player vision and reaction in attack and defence; to increase awareness of marking and danger zones, and how to overcome them

Practice set-up: Players work in pairs. Four markers are set out to create a square grid 10 m x 10 m, with a pitch line running across the centre. Player A has possession of the ball, and player B just has a stick. Player A moves anywhere between the markers on his side of the line, and player B mirrors the moves exactly. If player A moves to his left then player B moves to his right and so on. Player A can move forwards, backwards, sideways and change direction and speed as much as he wants. Player A scores a point if he can get the ball over the line and back again with his stick without player B gaining possession. It is essential that player B reacts quickly when player A approaches the line in order to gain possession. Allow play to continue until both players have had a chance to play with possession of the ball.

Equipment: A stick for each player and a ball for each pair; six markers

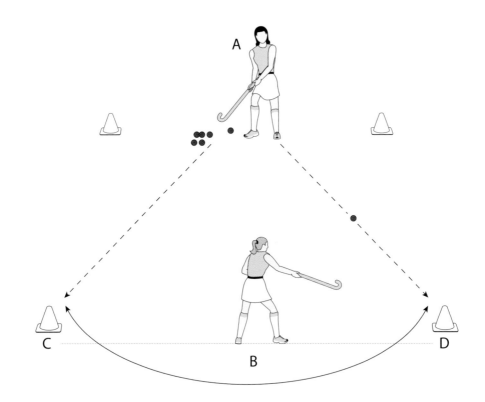

Purpose: To practise intercepting the ball on front and reverse stick; to anticipate your opponent's actions and stop the intended pass

Practice set-up: Four markers are set up in a grid of approximately six metres wide and eight metres long. Players work in pairs and player A starts with a pool of six balls. Player A firmly pushes the first ball towards marker D. The player at B should be able to take a stride and reach to collect the ball or slip step, stride and reach. Player at A then pushes the next ball to marker C, and Player B slip steps again and picks up on reverse stick, pulling the ball back and on to the front stick. By reaching slightly forwards rather than straight across, the pull back is easy. Player A passes all six balls to player B, and then play reverses.

Equipment: A stick for each player and six balls; four markers

Progression: A can pass to either side and B has to read the move to intercept; instead of a push use a sweep.

SHOOTING AT GOAL

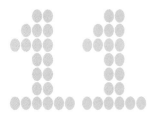

It is not always the hardest hit ball, or the ball hit with the longest swing that ends up in the net. The ball just needs to cross the line and is often put in from a close position. Goalkeeper practices are a big help here to allow players to practise shots from several areas of the circle.

Crossed from the right and the ball beats the keeper and defender, but not the lively attacker at the back post who just pops it in the net.

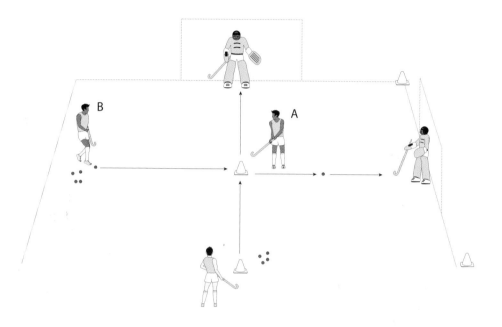

Purpose: To practise picking up and shooting around the penalty spot

Practice set-up: Three players and two goalkeepers are assigned to each grid. Using the corner of the pitch place the markers as indicated to create a square 18 x 18 m. Two goals are placed on the line, halfway between the markers. One marker is placed in the centre of the square to indicate the position of player A. Players B and C have a pool of five balls each. Player B passes to player A who picks up and shoots at either goal. Player C then takes a turn to feed to player A. Both goalkeepers must watch every ball and be prepared to make a save as the striker can change direction. After 10 shots at goal have been taken, the players change scorer and repeat.

Equipment: A stick for each player; 10 balls, seven markers and two goals

Progression: Instead of a flat pass, players must use a bounce pass, which often happens in this area as the ball comes off a defender's stick.

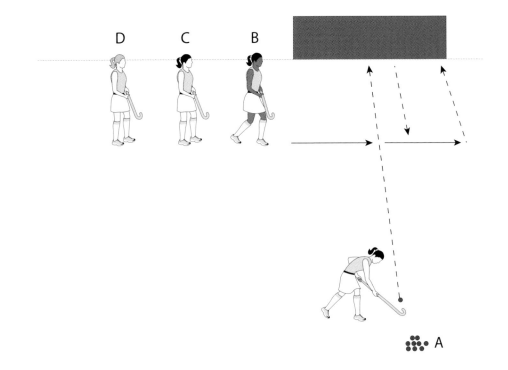

Purpose: To practise rebounding the ball on front and reverse stick

Practice set-up: Four players are assigned to each grid. Player A starts with a pool of 10 balls opposite the rebound board, with the others standing in a line at right angles to the path of the ball. Player A firmly pushes the first ball to the board. Player B steps forwards and stretches to pick up the ball on the rebound, and in the next stride slides it back into goal around the 'goalkeeper'. This should not be a big swing movement – just step, reach and pick up, step and push into goal. Return to start while A feeds the next ball to player B and so on. Once all 10 passes have been made, players swap position and repeat as before.

Equipment: A stick for each player and 10 balls; a rebound board (you can use a goal sideboard or backboard for this by turning the goal round).

Progression: Players run from right to left and the scoring shot is on the reverse.

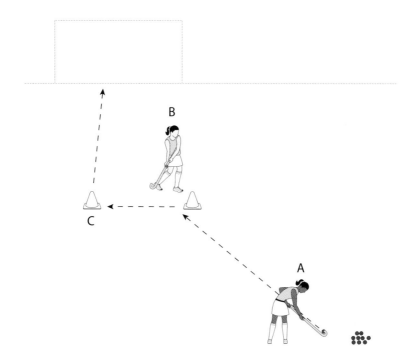

Purpose: To practise an easy reverse hit (this can be used all over the field but is something players like to try in the circle)

Practice set-up: Players work in pairs. Player A starts with a pool of 10 balls, and firmly pushes the first ball to player B, who is in line with the right post and about 5 metres out. Player B collects the ball and plays it across the goal towards marker C. Player B then steps with their right foot towards the ball, reaches and sweeps the ball into goal with a flat stick and hands together at the top of the stick, which is low to the ground. The ball should be hit by the front edge and should stay flat. Once all 10 shots have been made the players swap positions and repeat.

Equipment: A stick for each player and 10 balls; one goal for each pair (you can use markers to mark out the goal if necessary)

Progression: Players can move further away from the goal so that the need for accuracy is increased.

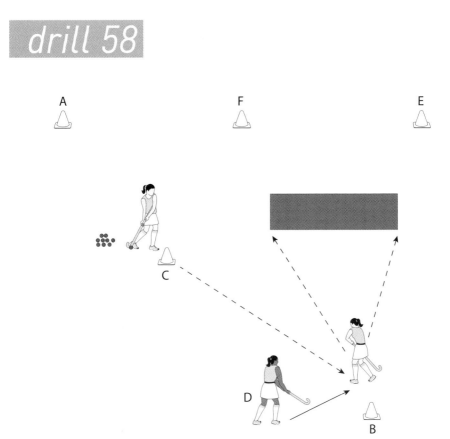

Purpose: To give players the confidence to perform the basic elements of the penalty corner routine – pass, control and shoot

Practice set-up: Three players are assigned to each grid. Place a marker at E, take four strides and place one at F (to represent the goal). From F, walk out 10 strides to place a marker A, and from the centre of the goal walk forwards 16 strides and place a marker at B. These indicate the push out and stop points. Place a marker at C halfway along line AB. Place a rebound board nine metres from B so if the player hits the board, it is the equivalent of a goal.

The player at C has a pool of 10 balls, and passes the first ball easily to be stopped by the player at B. Player D moves in to pull the ball forwards and send the shot to the rebound board. Once the player at C has passed all 10 balls to B, the players swap positions and repeat as above.

Equipment: A stick for each player and 10 balls; rebound board and five markers

GAME SCENARIOS

It is essential that practices develop to be as near to real game scenarios as possible. Defenders can be added, and drills can be speeded up to make things more realistic. Always try to incorporate skills into a practice session that will be transferable to a real game.

Just when it looks like getting away from him, Christopher Zeller (Germany) uses his reach and strong right arm to bring the ball back under his control, while still motoring along.

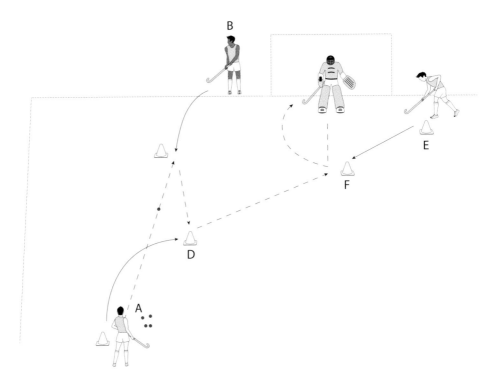

Purpose: To get the ball into the circle from the left using the player on the end line

Practice set-up: Three players and one goalkeeper are assigned to each grid. Player A starts with a pool of five balls, and pushes the first ball firmly up the wing and inwards to the marker placed 3 metres away from the end line. Player A follows the pass but stays wide so that they can run in to the return pass, making it easier to pass to player E. Player B waits on the end line and then goes rapidly to collect the ball.

Player B picks up and plays the ball straight back to marker D. Player A runs on to the ball, passing to the penalty spot at marker F for player E to deflect into goal or pick up and shoot. This does require timing, and players should run through it slowly at first to get the pattern right.

Equipment: A stick for each player and five balls; a goal and five markers

Progression: Dummy defenders can be added gradually to increase the need for accurate passing and shooting, and also increase the pressure on players.

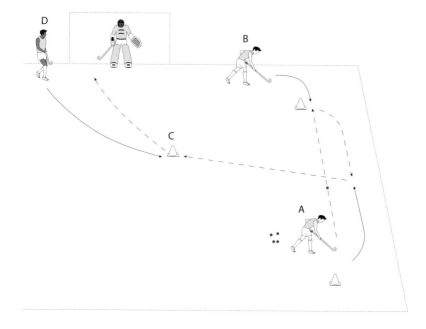

Purpose: To get the ball into the circle from the right using the player on the end line

Practice set-up: Four players and one goalkeeper are assigned to each grid. Player A has a pool of five balls and passes the first one up the wing, and wide of the marker that is placed 3 m from the end line. Player A follows the line of the ball, but stays wide. Player B, positioned at the end line, goes forwards quickly, collects the pass and plays it back towards player A. Player A collects the ball again and passes it to the penalty spot at C for player D (also starting on the end line) to deflect the ball into goal or pick up and shoot. This does require timing and should be run through slowly at first to gain the pattern.

Equipment: A stick for each player and five balls; three markers and a goal

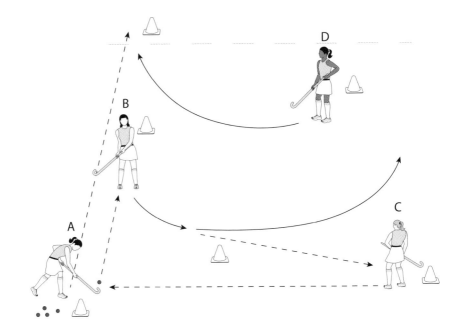

Purpose: To get the ball moving on the left of the back or midfield

Practice set-up: This drill should be played in the area from 22 m to the halfway line across the middle of the pitch. Place the markers as indicated on the diagram. Four players are assigned to each grid. Player A has a pool of five balls, and passes the first one firmly up the wing to player B, who collects the ball on the run, and passes it to player C before continuing in-field. Player C passes wide left back to A, who then passes down the wing to player D, through the space left by player B. Player D, who has run wide, collects the ball. In a match, player D would continue into attack down the wing, supported by player A running behind and player B from the right.

Equipment: A stick for each player and five balls; six markers

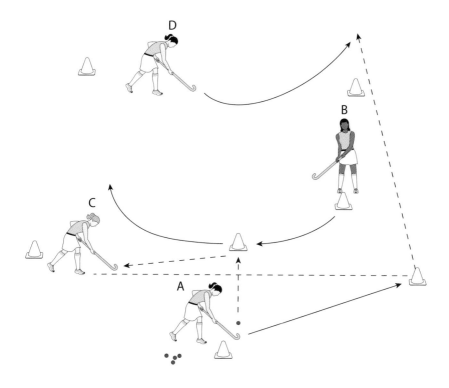

Purpose: To get the ball moving forwards on the right of the back or midfield

Practice set-up: This drill should be played in the area from 22 m to the halfway line across the middle of the pitch. Place the markers as indicated on the diagram. Four players are assigned to each grid. Player A has a pool of five balls, and passes the first one firmly up the wing to player B, who collects the ball on the run, and passes it to player C before continuing in-field. Player C passes wide right back to A, who then passes down the wing to player D, through the space left by player B. Player D, who has run wide, collects the ball. In a match, player D would continue into attack down the wing, supported by A running behind and B from the left.

Equipment: A stick for each player and five balls; six markers

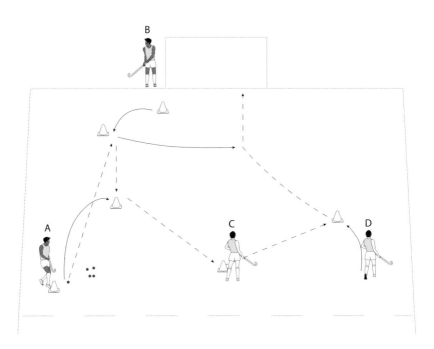

Purpose: To teach players to link by moving the ball across field via the midfield players

Practice set-up: This drill should be played across the full width of the pitch from the goal line out to the 22m line. Four players are assigned to each grid. Player A passes the ball to the front to player B, and follows the line of the ball but stays wide. Player B comes in from the end line to collect the ball and passes it back to player A. Player A then passes inside to player C, and player C passes across to player D who has been moving forwards on the right side. Player D passes quickly to the penalty spot for player B to score. Repeat until all the balls have been used, and then switch the players in midfield around and repeat as above.

Equipment: A stick for each player and five balls; six markers and a goal

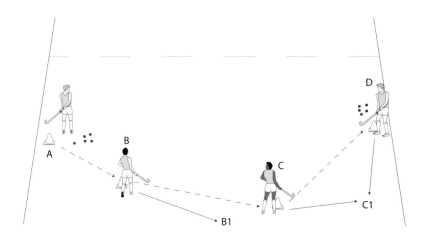

Purpose: To play the ball accurately across the pitch at the back line

Practice set-up: Four players are assigned to each grid. Players are placed by each marker in a curve, with the outside players slightly ahead of the central pair. Players A and D have a pool of five balls each. The first ball is passed through the players from A to D. Players should follow the line of the ball wide so that the return pass is easier, and there is support for the player on the ball. Once the ball reaches player D, they pass their first ball back along the line and so on until all the balls in the pool have been used.

Equipment: A stick for each player and 10 balls in two pools; four markers

Progression: All sorts of patterns can be developed from this movement, with the ball going A, B, C, D round the back or A, C, D or A, B, D or A, B, C, A.

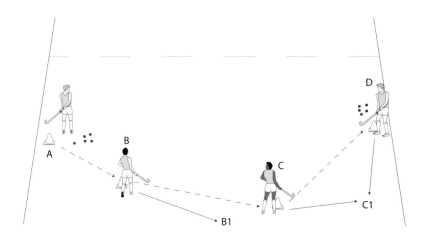

NO GO ZONE

Purpose: To encourage early accurate feeding from defence to attack, allowing for a break and shot

Practice set-up: Using the sideline and end line area 12 m wide and 22 m long, place the markers as indicated in the illustration. Ten players are split into two teams of five players – each team has three attackers and two defenders giving a 3 v 2 either side of the 'no-go zone'. Three attackers in team A start with the ball and try to score. If the defenders in team B gain possession they get a 'free pass' through the 'no-go zone' to the B attackers who try to score at the other end.

Any shots on goal score. Defenders then get the ball for a 'free pass' to their attackers. Shots missing goal don't score, and defenders collect a ball from the ball pool and play on.

Equipment: A stick for each player and one ball; 11 markers and two goals

Progression: Allow the attackers to continue when they lose possession; place one new player in the no-go zone who acts as a link between defence and strikers for both teams.

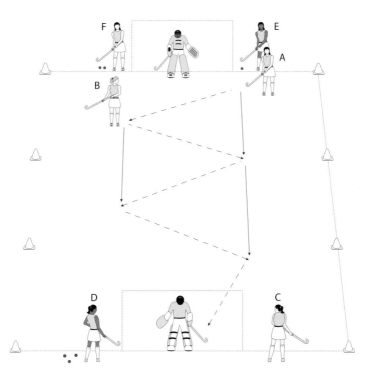

Purpose: To teach players to break away to get a shot at goal; to teach the goalkeeper to save in these situations

Practice set-up: Six players and two goalkeepers are assigned to each grid, with players working in pairs. Players A and B run forwards, interpassing as they go. As soon as they reach the last set of markers they can shoot. When the shot has been taken, players C and D break forwards with another ball going the other way. Players E and F then follow. Play continues until all pairs have attempted shooting at each goal.

Equipment: A stick for each player and six balls in two pools; eight markers and two goals

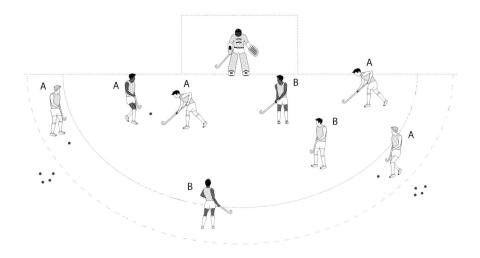

Purpose: To develop effective feeding into the circle; to encourage attackers to receive passes under pressure and to win shots at goal

Practice set-up: The players operate within the circle and the 5 m extra area. Players work in two teams with five attackers (in bibs) and three defenders. Three attackers work inside the circle and two work in the 5 m band outside the circle. Attackers outside can move around, pass between themselves and feed to the attackers inside but can't go inside themselves. The aim of the attackers inside is to shoot, score and rebound, and if they feel under pressure they can feed the ball to the attackers outside the circle to be fed back in.

The defenders can mark but are not able to tackle, so the passing should be strong. However, they can intercept the ball and pass it to their defender on the outside to score. To restart the game players can take a ball from the pool and continue as before.

Equipment: A stick for each player and one ball; a goal and five bibs for attackers

Progression: The defender outside the circle becomes live and can tackle the attackers on the outside.

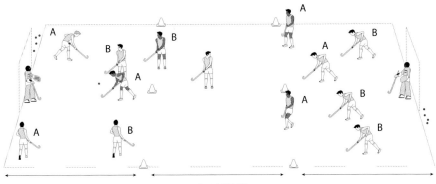

NO GO ZONE

Purpose: To teach players to sweep hit the ball long and quickly to the strikers (by-passing the midfield)

Practice set-up: This drill should be played in the area from the 22 m line to the halfway line, across the full width of the pitch. This should be divided into three sections, with the central section being about 15 m wide and becoming the 'no-go zone'. Twelve players and two goalkeepers are assigned to each grid, and the players are divided into two teams with different bib colours. Each area should have three attackers from one team, and one defender and two receivers from the other team. The receivers do not take part in the 3 v 1 game that goes on between the attackers and the defender – they only take part in the game if the defender wins the ball and feeds it to them, if the goalkeeper kicks a clearance to them or after the attackers have missed a goal (in these circumstances they can use a free ball from the ball pool).

Only one ball is in play at any one time, and attackers are not permitted to tackle receivers who are trying to get the ball through the no-go zone to their strikers. Receivers can pass between each other to get a better pass through the zone.

Equipment: A stick for each player and two ball pools beside the goals; six markers and two goals; 12 bibs (six of each in two colours)

drill 69

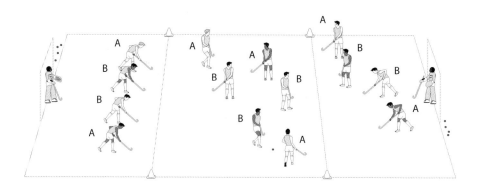

Purpose: To teach the players to create support for the attack, improving the chances of scoring

Practice set-up: This drill should be played in the area from the 22 m line to the goal line, across the full width of the pitch. This should be divided into three sections. Fourteen players and two goalkeepers are assigned to each grid, and the players are divided into two teams (teams A and B) with different bib colours. The area on the left should have two attackers from team A and two defenders from team B. The area on the right should have two attackers from team B and two defenders from team A. The central area should have three players from team A (two are designated to go into the left area to help their attackers, and one is designated to go into the right area to help their defenders. Team B also has three players in the central area, and the same arrangement exists. Players in the central area are allowed to carry the ball back into the central area. Two are designated to go into the right area to help their attackers and one is designated to go into the left area to help their defenders. Team A defend the left goal and score in the right goal, and vice versa. Attack is 4 v 3.

Equipment: A stick for each player and two ball pools beside the goals; four markers, two goals and 14 bibs (seven of each in two colours)

GOALKEEPING

Goalkeepers are so important now in the game that they have their own practices and top teams employ specialist coaches for this position. Goalkeepers are no longer just there to be a space filler between the posts. They are fit, flexible and work on dynamic exercises. Goalkeepers are possible match winners and can be heroes in both open play situations and at set piece plays. They must also know the game and be prepared to help organise the defence in front of them.

Modern protective kit has ensured that they are as safe as possible but it must always be worn fully when they are at practice. Goalkeepers will save far more shots in practice than they do in a match so their chances of injury will be increased. In some instances goalkeepers use extra padding in practice.

The good news for the attacking players is that they can practise skills against these goalkeepers while they are helping the goalkeeper with their practice. All the drills in this section can be helpful to outfield players who could end up in scoring positions. During these practices, good technique should be demanded from the goalkeepers, for example, the clearance should not give away a careless penalty corner by a poor kick either high or direct to an attacker. Hits in these practices should not be wild full-blooded swings but controlled and accurate firm hits.

In all multiple player shooting practices players must be aware of the shooting order, both for their own safety and for the safety of the goalkeepers. Run these patterns through slowly the first time to allow everyone to position themselves safely. Thought should also be given by the coach to placing the players and choosing the type of shot.

Indian GK Dipika Murty stretches and dives in a 'must reach this or it is a goal' situation against Kim De Haas (Netherlands Antilles)

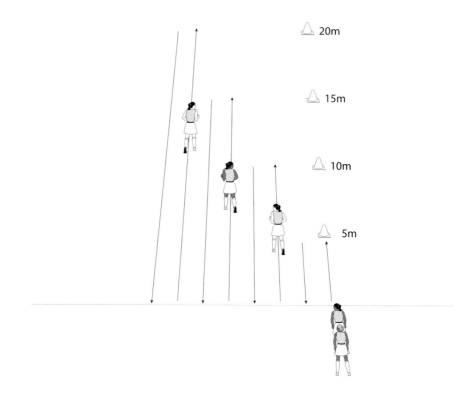

Purpose: To develop the capacity of players to accelerate forwards rapidly

Practice set-up: Set out the markers at 5 m increments up to 20 m. On the start signal the first player accelerates as fast as possible to each of the cones and walks back to the start point. One set will be completed when the player runs to all of the markers up to the 20 m cone then back down to the 5m marker (seven sprints).

Equipment: Four markers

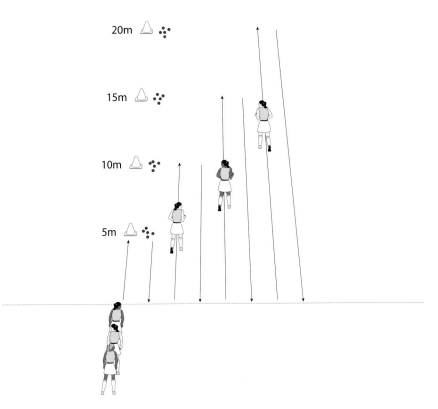

Purpose: To develop the capacity of players to accelerate forwards rapidly, before kicking a ball away on reaching the cone

Practice set-up: Set out the markers at 5 m increments up to 20 m (as in drill 70). On the start signal the first player accelerates as fast as possible to each of the cones and walks back to the start point. One set will be completed when the player runs to all of the cones up to the 20 m marker then back down to the 5 m marker (seven sprints). On reaching the marker the player kicks a ball.

Equipment: Four markers and a pool of balls at each marker; a harness or resistance band for the progression

Progression: Players work in pairs and repeat as before, but this time both players take it in turns to resist the other by tying a harness to his partner. The player who provides the resistance must vary the amount on each run.

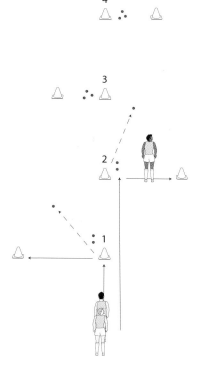

Purpose: To develop acceleration capacity and lateral movement

Practice set-up: Set out the markers at 5 m increments up to 20 m (as in the previous drill) and place four markers 3–5 m out to the sides. On the start signal the player sprints to marker 1, kicks the ball then slip steps to the left before walking back to the start point.

 The player repeats the above, but this time sprinting to marker 2, kicking the ball and slip stepping to the right before returning to the start point. After all four markers have been reached it is the turn of the next player.

Equipment: Eight markers and a pool of balls at each marker

Tip: Make sure the players are balanced to drive sideways as soon as they have kicked the ball.

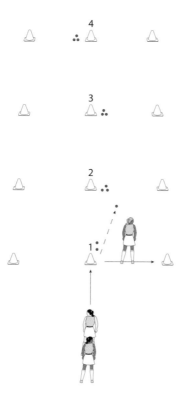

Purpose: To develop acceleration capacity, lateral movement and visual reactions

Practice set-up: Set out four markers at 5 m increments up to 20 m (as in drill 72) and place eight markers 3–5 m out to the sides. On the start signal the player sprints to marker 1, kicks the ball then looks for a hand signal from the coach then slip steps right or left accordingly. The player then walks back to the start point, and repeats the above but this time sprinting to marker 2. After all four markers have been reached it is the turn of the next player.

Equipment: Twelve markers and a pool of balls at each marker

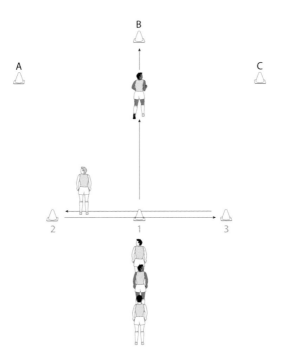

Purpose: To develop the ability to rapidly change direction

Practice set-up: Set out three markers in a straight line and 3–4 m apart, as well as a further three markers 5–10 m away and 4–6 m apart. The first player starts at the centre marker and slip steps to marker 2 then to marker 3 and back to the centre. On reaching the centre the player then sprints to one of the markers A, B or C before returning to the start.

Equipment: Six markers

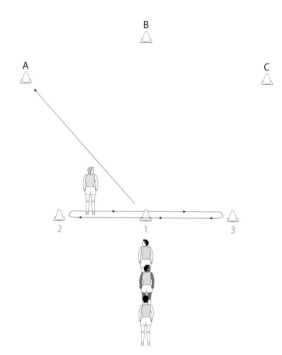

Purpose: To develop the ability to rapidly change direction, improve lateral movement and react to an audible cue

Practice set-up: Set out three markers in a straight line and 3–4 m apart, as well as a further three markers 5–10 m away and 4–6 m apart. The first player starts at the centre marker and slip steps to marker 2 then to marker 3 and back to the centre and keeps this going until the coach shouts 'A', 'B' or 'C'. On hearing this, the player must immediately react and run to the corresponding marker before returning to the start.

Equipment: Six markers

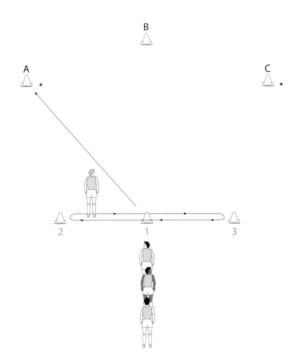

Purpose: To develop the ability to rapidly change direction and react to an audible cue

Practice set-up: Set out three markers in a straight line and 3–4 m apart, as well as a further three markers 5–10 m away and 4–6 m apart. A ball is placed at markers A, B and C. The first player starts at the centre marker and slip steps to marker 2 then to marker 3 and back to the centre and keeps this going until the coach shouts 'A', 'B' or 'C'. On hearing this, the player must immediately react and run to the corresponding marker, and kick a ball before returning to the start.

Equipment: Six markers and a pool of balls at each marker

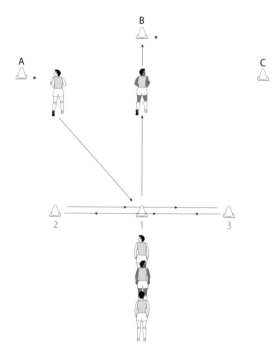

Purpose: To develop the ability to rapidly change direction and react to an audible cue

Practice set-up: Set out three markers in a straight line and 3–4 m apart, as well as a further three markers 5–10 m away and 4–6 m apart. A ball is placed at markers A, B and C. The first player starts at the centre marker and slip steps to marker 2 then to marker 3 and back to the centre and keeps this going until the coach shouts 'A', 'B' or 'C'. On hearing this, the player must immediately react and run to the corresponding marker, and kick a ball. Having kicked the ball the player makes his way back to the start point as fast as possible while reverse running.

Equipment: Six markers and a pool of balls at each marker

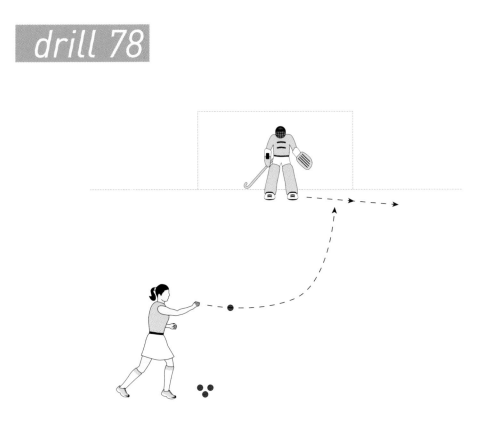

Purpose: To develop hand–eye ball co-ordination, lateral movement and lower reach and visual reaction times

Practice set-up: Use an actual goal mouth or one set up with markers. The coach stands at varying distances from the player and rapidly feeds balls at the goal mouth trying to score a goal (rolling the balls along the ground at various speeds and angles). The balls are collected and re-used until either a time limit has expired or all the balls are dispersed and unable to be collected by the coach. The goalkeeper has to prevent a goal being scored by using the foot or the hand. Any number of balls may be used.

Equipment: A goal and up to 20 tennis or hockey balls

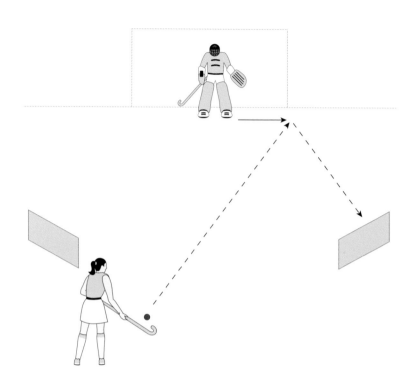

Purpose: To gain confidence when saving and clearing

Practice set-up: A player feeds balls towards the goalkeeper from the penalty spot, passing the first ball a metre to the goalkeeper's left side. The goalkeeper should clear the ball along the ground with their left foot to the left rebound board and then return to the centre of goal by slip step action.

The player then passes the next ball a metre to the goalkeeper's right side and the goalkeeper should clear the ball along the ground with their right foot to the right rebound board and then return to the centre of goal by slip step action. Repeat the above for all 10 balls and then allow the goalkeeper to rest while the player reassembles the balls. Players can pass by hand or using stick depending on how competent they are.

Equipment: Ten balls; two rebound boards (or four markers) and a goal

Progression: Progress to making a bounce pass to the goalkeeper, and then a volley below the knee.

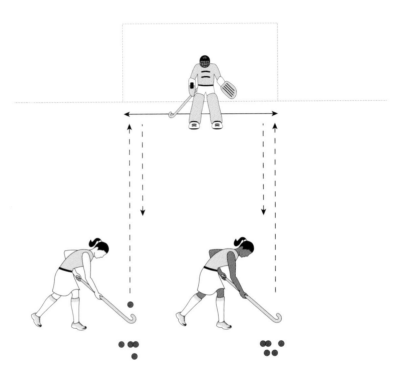

Purpose: To gain confidence when saving and clearing

Practice set-up: Two players (level with the penalty spot and just inside the line of the post) take turns to feed balls towards the goalkeeper. Player A passes the first ball just inside the goalkeeper's right post. The goalkeeper moves across and clears along the ground with their right foot back to the feeder, and returns to the centre of goal by slip step action. Player B then passes the next ball just inside the goalkeeper's left post. The goalkeeper moves across and clears along the ground with their left foot back to the feeder, and returns to the centre of goal by slip step action. Repeat the above for all 10 balls and then allow the goalkeeper to rest while the players reassemble the balls. Players can pass by hand or using stick depending on how competent they are.

Equipment: Ten balls and a goal

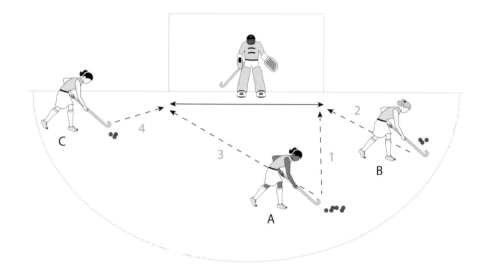

Purpose: To gain confidence when saving a shot, then a rebound, and clearing

Practice set-up: Three players are positioned to feed to the goalkeeper. Player A has a pool of six balls, and players B and C have a pool of three balls each. Player A feeds the first ball flat to the goalkeeper's left post (pass 1). The goalkeeper saves and then saves a flat shot from player B (pass 2) and clears by foot.

Player A then feeds the second ball flat across to the far post (pass 3). The goalkeeper saves and then saves another flat shot from player C (pass 4) before clearing by foot. Repeat the above for all 12 balls and then allow the goalkeeper to rest while the players reassemble the balls. Players can pass by hand or using stick depending on how competent they are.

Equipment: Twelve balls and a goal

Progression: Still keeping the pass from player A flat, allow the rebound shots from players B and C to be lifted; player A can lift the shot as a volley below the knee, or progress to lifting the pass to below waist height.

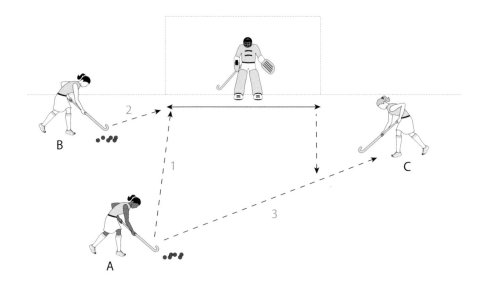

Purpose: To gain confidence when saving a shot, then a rebound, and clearing

Practice set-up: Three players are positioned to feed the goalkeeper, and players A and B have a pool of six balls each. Player A feeds the first ball flat to the goalkeeper's right post (pass 1). The goalkeeper saves and then saves a flat shot from player B (pass 2) before clearing by foot.

Player A then feeds the second ball flat across to the left post (pass 3) towards player C who moves forwards for a deflection towards the left post. The goalkeeper saves before clearing by foot. Repeat the above for all 12 balls and then allow the goalkeeper to rest while the players reassemble the balls.

Equipment: A stick for each player and 12 balls; a goal

drill 83

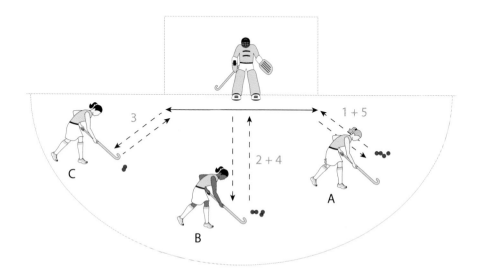

Purpose: To gain confidence when saving a shot, then a rebound, and clearing

Practice set-up: Players A and B have a pool of four balls each; player C has two balls. Player A feeds the first ball flat to the goalkeeper's left post (pass 1), the goalkeeper saves and clears the ball back to player A. Player B now feeds flat, straight and easily towards the goal (pass 2). The goalkeeper runs to kick return the ball to player B, before moving to the right post to save and return the incoming pass from player C (pass 3). Player B again sends a ball flat, straight and gently towards the goal (pass 4) and the goalkeeper again runs towards it and kicks it back. Player A then completes series with a shot to the left post, which the goalkeeper clears back. Repeat the above to give a set of 10 shots, and then allow the goalkeeper to rest while the players reassemble the balls.

Equipment: A stick for each player and 10 balls; a goal

Progression: Allow the passes to be bounced to the goalkeeper; players A and C can lift the pass to any height, but player B can only play it flat or bounced so that the goalkeeper can practise the kick moving into the ball coming towards him.

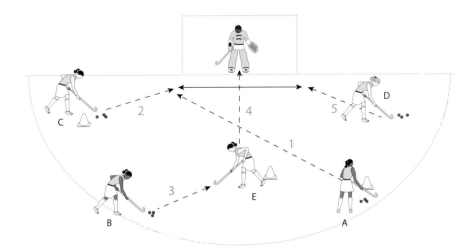

Purpose: To gain confidence when saving a shot, then a rebound, and clearing

Practice set-up: Five players are positioned to feed the goalkeeper, and players A, B, C and D have three balls each. Player A hits the first ball flat to the goal-keeper's right post (pass 1). The goalkeeper saves, and then saves a flat shot from player C (pass 2) and clears by foot. Player B now hits flat across to the left post to player E coming forwards for a deflection. The goalkeeper saves, and again saves a flat shot from player D before clearing by foot. Repeat the above for all 12 balls, and then allow the goalkeeper to rest while the players reassemble the balls.

Equipment: A stick for each player and 12 balls; a goal

Progression: Players C and D can lift their shots, but hits from players A and B should be controlled and flat.

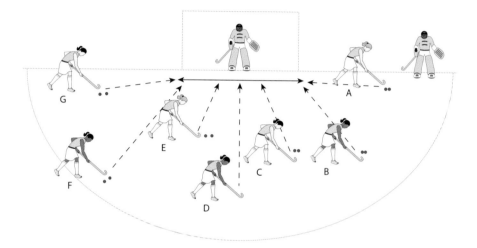

Purpose: To gain confidence when saving a series of shots

Practice set-up: Seven players are positioned to feed the goalkeeper, and each player has two balls. The players take it in turns to shoot from player A through to player G, using their stipulated shot. Players A and G use a flat push; players B and F use a flat hit; players C and E use a bounce ball and player D uses a flat hit straight. Allow each player to have two shots each, and then swap over the goalkeeper while the players reassemble the balls.

Equipment: A stick for each player and 14 balls; a goal

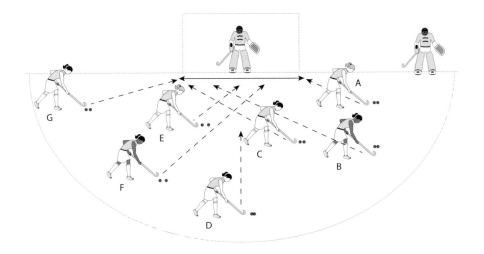

Purpose: To gain confidence when saving a series of shots from various points in the circle

Practice set-up: Seven players are positioned to feed the goalkeeper, and each player has two balls. The players take it in turns to shoot from player A through to player G, using their stipulated shot. Player A uses a high flick to the left post; player B uses a flat hit to the right post; player C uses a knee high flick to the right post; player D uses a flat hit to the middle of the goal; player E uses a flick at knee height to the left post; player F uses a flat hit to the left post and player G uses a high flick to the right post.

Allow each player to have two shots each, and then swap over the goalkeeper while the players reassemble the balls.

Equipment: A stick for each player and 14 balls; a goal

RELAY RACES

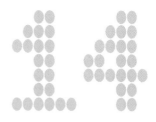

Relay races are a fun and enjoyable method of training a squad of players. The relay race format cultivates the competitive nature of the players once the correct movements have been mastered. It is important that the correct technique does not suffer due to the players' desire to win. It must be re-enforced by the coach that only correct execution of the drill will suffice and that disqualification or time penalties may be enforced.

Two minds think alike and two bodies have a close encounter. Christa Cullen (England) and Nuria Camon (Spain) tango for possession.

25m

50m

Purpose: To develop pace and competitiveness

Practice set-up: Split players up into teams of 4–6. Using the 25 m and 50 m lines, deploy half the team on the 25 m line and the remaining half on the 50 m line directly opposite their team mates. Use a bib as a 'baton'. On the whistle the race starts with the teams' first player sprinting and passing the bib to the second player, who sprints towards the third and so on until all players have run once each.

If one or two teams consistently dominate, rearrange the teams to ensure an even spread of fast runners across the teams.

Equipment: A bib for each team

Purpose: To develop pace, agility and competitiveness

Practice set-up: Split players up into teams of 4–6. Using the 25 m and 50 m lines, deploy half the team on the 25 m line and the remaining half on the 50 m line directly opposite their team mates. Use a bib as a 'baton'. On the whistle the race starts with the teams' first player sprinting and passing the bib to the second player, who sprints towards the third and so on until all players have run once each. The players must perform four lateral jumps over a small 15 cm micro hurdle. If one or two teams consistently dominate, rearrange the teams to ensure an even spread of fast runners across the teams.

Equipment: A bib and micro hurdle for each team

Purpose: To develop pace, agility and competitiveness

Practice set-up: Split players up into teams of 4–6. Using the 25 m and 50 m lines, deploy half the team on the 25 m line and the remaining half on the 50 m line directly opposite their team mates.

With the stick and ball, the players take the ball to the micro hurdle then 'scoop' the ball over and take it to the next player in the team and so on until all players have performed this task. If one or two teams consistently dominate, rearrange the teams.

Equipment: A stick for each player and a ball for each team; micro hurdles

Purpose: To develop pace and competitiveness

Practice set-up: Split players up into teams of 4–6. Using the 25 m and 50 m lines, deploy half the team on the 25 m line and the remaining half on the 50 m line directly opposite their team mates. Use a bib as a 'baton'. On the whistle the race starts with the teams' first player sprinting and passing the bib to the second player, who sprints towards the third and so on until all players have run once each. The players perform fast feet drills through the lattes as illustrated – one footfall between each latte.

If one or two teams consistently dominate, rearrange the teams.

Equipment: One bib and 6–8 lattes per team

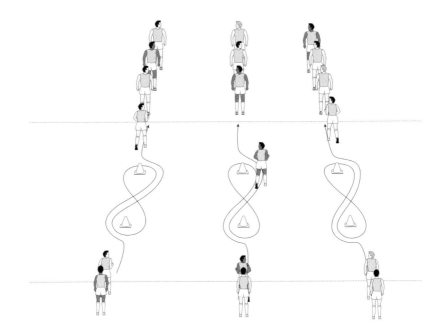

Purpose: To develop pace and competitiveness

Practice set-up: Split players up into teams of 4–6. Using the 25 m and 50 m lines, deploy half the team on the 25 m line and the remaining half on the 50 m line directly opposite their team mates. Use a bib as a 'baton'. On the whistle the race starts with the teams' first player sprinting and passing the bib to the second player, who sprints towards the third and so on until all players have run once each. The players perform the figure of eight around the markers in their path as illustrated. If one or two teams consistently dominate, rearrange the teams.

Equipment: One bib and two markers per team

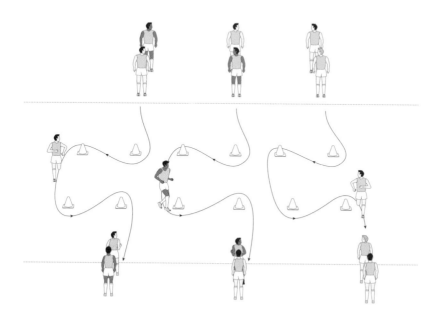

Purpose: To develop pace, agility and competitiveness

Practice set-up: Split players up into teams of 4–6. Using the 25 m and 50 m lines, deploy half the team on the 25 m line and the remaining half on the 50 m line directly opposite their team mates. Use a bib as a 'baton'. On the whistle the race starts with the teams' first player sprinting and passing the bib to the second player, who sprints towards the third and so on until all players have run once each. The players perform the loop as illustrated round the outside of the markers in their path. If one or two teams consistently dominate, rearrange the teams.

Equipment: One bib and four markers per team

drill 93

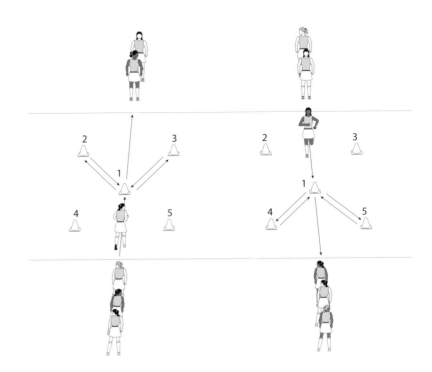

Purpose: To develop agility, pace and competitiveness

Practice set-up: Split players up into teams of 4–6. Using the 25 m and 50 m lines, deploy half the team on the 25 m line and the remaining half on the 50 m line directly opposite their team mates. Use a bib as a 'baton'. On the whistle the race starts with the teams' first player sprinting and passing the bib to the second player, who sprints towards the third and so on until all players have run once each. The players run to marker 1, then run diagonally left to marker 2, reverse run back to marker 1, run diagonally right to marker 3, reverse run to marker 1 and then sprint to pass the bib to the next player. The second runner uses markers 1, 4 and 5. If one or two teams consistently dominate, rearrange the teams.

Equipment: One bib and two markers per team

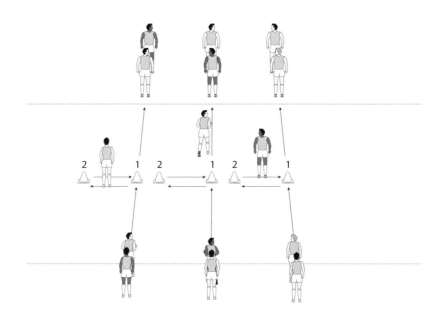

Purpose: To develop agility, pace and competitiveness

Practice set-up: Split players up into teams of 4–6. Using the 25 m and 50 m lines, deploy half the team on the 25 m line and the remaining half on the 50 m line directly opposite their team mates. Use a bib as a 'baton'. On the whistle the race starts with the teams' first players sprinting and passing the bib to the second player, who sprints towards the third and so on until all players have run once each.

The players slip step from marker 1 to 2, back to marker 1 then sprint as illustrated. If one or two teams consistently dominate, rearrange the teams.

Equipment: One bib and two markers per team

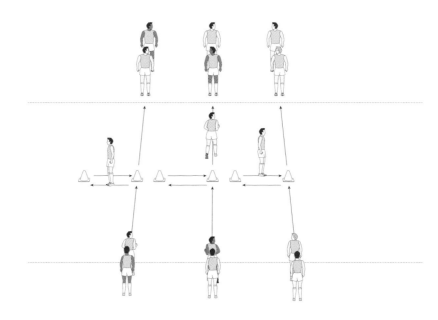

Purpose: To develop agility, pace and competitiveness

Practice set-up: Split players up into teams of three, two at one end and one at the other. Use half the zone of the previous relays. Use a bib as a 'baton'. On the whistle the race starts with the teams' first player sprinting and passing the bib to the second player, who sprints towards the third and so on until all players have run once each. The players sprint between the markers as illustrated.

Equipment: One bib and two markers per team

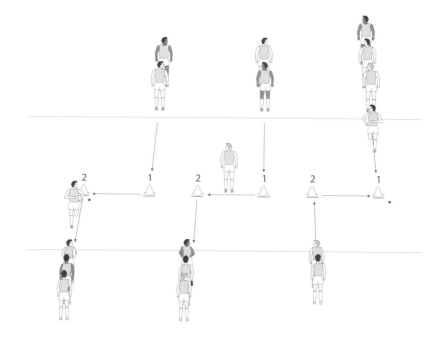

Purpose: To develop agility, pace and competitiveness

Practice set-up: Split players up into teams of 4–6. Using the 25 m and 50 m lines, deploy half the team on the 25 m line and the remaining half on the 50 m line directly opposite their team mates. Use a bib as a 'baton'. On the whistle the race starts with the teams' first players sprinting and passing the bibs to the second player, who sprints towards the third and so on until all players have run once each.

The players are required to pick up a ball from marker 1, and place it at marker 2. The next player replaces the ball at marker 1. If one or two teams consistently dominate, rearrange the teams.

Equipment: One bib, two markers and one ball per team

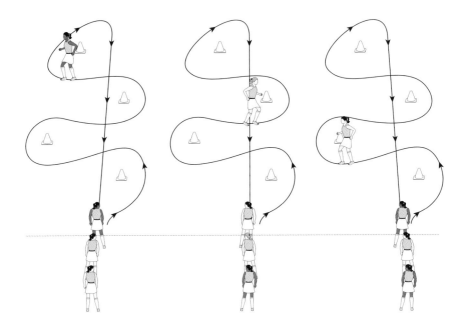

Purpose: To develop fast movements within a restricted area

Practice set-up: Split the players up into teams of 4–6. Set up the markers as indicated 2–3 m apart. Players weave their way to the last marker, then sprint back as illustrated. The bib is then passed to the next player until the whole team has completed the task.

Equipment: One bib and four markers per team

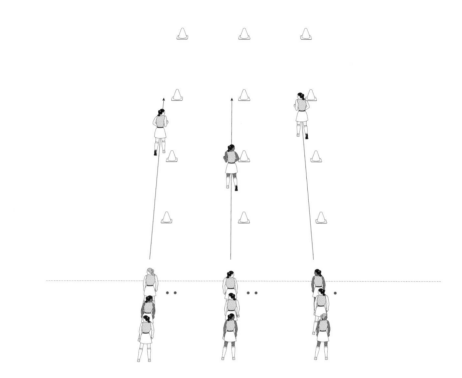

Purpose: To develop fast movement within a restricted area; to teach players how to stay low, pick up a ball and change direction rapidly in a competitive environment

Practice set-up: Split the players up into teams of 4–6. Set up the markers as indicated 2–3 m apart and in a straight line. Place four balls at the start point. The first player picks up one ball, runs to marker 1 and places the ball beside the marker. The player then returns to the start to pick up another ball, then runs to place it at marker 2, and repeats to place ball 3 at marker 3 and ball 4 at marker 4. The second player runs to marker 1 to bring ball 1 back to the start point, then returns each ball in turn. The third player puts them out again, and so on. Rotate the players so that they all perform collecting and replacing at different markers.

Equipment: Four markers and four hockey balls/tennis balls/bean bags per team

Got it! Nice jab tackle by Olivia Georgina (Spain) wins the ball from Mandy Haas (Germany) and could set up an attacking 2 v 1 situation from a 2 v 1 defensive situation.

WARMING DOWN

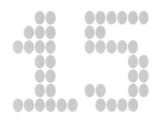

The purpose of the warm-down is to start the post match/training recovery process. A correctly executed warm-down will assist in clearing the toxin build-up from the muscles. Light physical activity combined with stretching and mobility exercises will assist greatly in this process. The players can start the warm-down with some simple jogging – you can also use the following drills, as long as they are undertaken gently by the players.

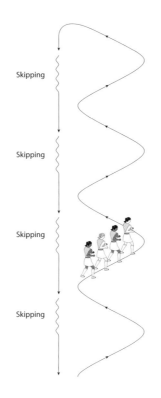

Skipping

Skipping

Skipping

Skipping

Practice set-up: Following the principles set out in drill 13, the players simply move through the markers slowly performing the movements. Care must be taken to ensure that the intensity is maintained at an appropriate low level.

Split the players into teams of 4. Players stand behind each other in a line, and the lead player moves the group forward at a jogging pace in a zig-zag pattern across the pitch with easy bend and push off the outside foot when changing direction. Jog straight back across the pitch with short spells of low skipping.

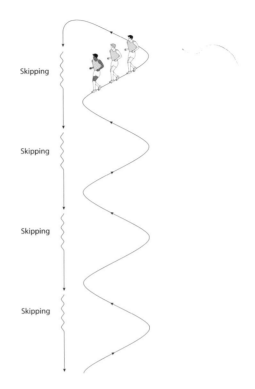

Skipping

Skipping

Skipping

Skipping

Practice set-up: As in drill 99 but alternating jogging with reverse skipping. Care must be taken when travelling in reverse not to step on the marker and fall over. Remember that the players will be experiencing post session/match fatigue.

As in drill 99, split the players into teams of 4. Players stand behind each other in a line, and the lead player moves the group forward at a jogging pace in a zig-zag pattern across the pitch. This time players should jog forwards on the left diagonal, and reverse skip on the right diagonal. Jog straight back across the pitch with short spells of low skipping.

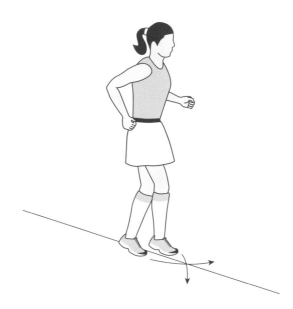

Practice set-up: Using the markings on the pitch, the players jog on top of the lines. The players place their right foot on the left of the line and their left foot on the right of the line.